The First-Year Experience
Monograph Series No. 41

The 2003 National Survey on First-Year Seminars

Continuing Innovations in the Collegiate Curriculum

Barbara F. Tobolowsky

with Marla Mamrick and Bradley E. Cox

ESOURCE CENTER FOR THE FIRST-YEAR EXPERIENCE®
& STUDENTS IN TRANSITION
IIVERSITY OF SOUTH CAROLINA, 2005

Cite as:

Tobolowsky, B. F. (2005). *The 2003 national survey on first-year seminars: Continuing innovations in the collegiate curriculum* (Monograph No. 41). Columbia, SC: University of South Carolina, National Resource Center for The First-Year Experience and Students in Transition.

Sample chapter citation:

Mamrick, M. (2005). The first-year seminar: An historical perspective. In B. F. Tobolowsky, *The 2003 national survey on first-year seminars: Continuing innovations in the collegiate curriculum* (Monograph No. 41) (pp. 15-20). Columbia, SC: University of South Carolina, National Resource Center for The First-Year Experience and Students in Transition.

Additional copies of this monograph may be ordered from the National Resource Center for The First-Year Experience and Students in Transition, University of South Carolina, 1728 College Street, Columbia, SC 29208. Telephone (803) 777-6229. Fax (803) 777-4699.

Special gratitude is expressed to Jenny Anderson, Composition Assistant, for design; to Michelle Mouton, Editorial Assistant, for copyediting and layout; to Inge Lewis, Editor, for proofing assistance; and to Tracy L. Skipper, Editorial Projects Coordinator, for copyediting.

ISBN: 1-889271-49-7

Tobolowsky, Barbara F.
 The 2003 National Survey on First-Year Seminars: continuing innovations in the curriculum / Barbara F. Tobolowsky with Marla Mamrick and Bradley E. Cox.
    p. cm. -- (The first year experience monograph series ; no. 41)
  ISBN 1-889271-49-7
 1. College student development programs--United States--Evaluation. 2. Cc
United States. 3. Seminars--United States--Evaluation. 4. National Survey of
Programming. 5. Educational surveys--United States. I. Mamrick, Marla. II.
National Resource Center for the First-Year Experience & Students in Transi
South Carolina) IV. Title. V. Series.
 LB2343.4.T55 2005
 378.1'98--dc22
                              2004025509

Contents

List of Tables...5

Foreword
Betsy O. Barefoot...9

Introduction
Barbara F. Tobolowsky..11

Chapter 1
The First-Year Seminar: An Historical Perspective
Marla Mamrick...15

Chapter 2
Survey Methodology...21

Chapter 3
A Two-Year and Four-Year Institutional Comparison......23

Chapter 4
aching in First-Year Seminars................................33

er 5
ment and the First-Year Seminar.........................37

6
orations Into Today's First-Year Seminar.........41

Survey Responses
....47

4

Chapter 8
Summary of Selected Findings.................................*93*

Appendix A
Survey Instrument.................................*99*

Appendix B
*Respondents to the 2003 National Survey on
First-Year Seminars*.................................*107*

Appendix C
Proprietary Institutions.................................*123*

About the Contributors.................................*125*

List of Tables

Table 2.1 *Representation of 2003 Survey Respondents Compared to National Average by Institutional Type and Size* 22

Table 3.1 *Undergraduate Headcount at Two-Year Institutions* 23

Table 3.2 *Undergraduate Headcount at Four-Year Institutions* 24

Table 3.3 *Percentage of First-Year Students Who Take the Seminar at Two-Year Institutions* 24

Table 3.4 *Type of First-Year Seminars at Two-Year Institutions* 25

Table 3.5 *Percentage of First-Year Students who Take the Seminar at Four-Year Institutions* 25

Table 3.6 *Type of First-Year Seminars at Four-Year Institutions* 26

Table 3.7 *Percentage of Two-Year Institutions That Require First-Year Seminars* 27

Table 3.8 *Percentage of Four-Year Institutions That Require First-Year Seminars* 28

Table 3.9 *Most Important Course Objectives at Two-Year Institutions* 30

Table 3.10 *Most Important Course Topics at Two-Year Institutions* 30

Table 3.11 *Most Important Course Objectives at Four-Year Institutions* 31

Table 3.12 *Most Important Course Topics at Four-Year Institutions* 32

Table 4.1 *Percentage of First-Year Seminar Sections That Were Team Taught* 33

Table 5.1 *Types of Evaluation Methods Used* 37

Table 5.2 *Outcomes Attributed to Participation in First-Year Seminars by Seminar Type* .. 38

Table 6.1 *Types of Courses Linked With the First-Year Seminar* 44

Table 7.1 *Characteristics of Responding Institutions With Seminars* 47

Table 7.2 *Seminar Longevity Across All Institutions* 48

Table 7.3 *Respondents Offering Each Type of Seminar Across All Institutions* 49

Table 7.4 *Percentage of Respondents Offering Each Type of Seminar by Institutional Affiliation* 49

Table 7.5 *Percentage of Respondents Offering Each Type of Seminar by Institutional Type* 50

Table 7.6 *Percentage of Respondents Offering Each Type of Seminar by Institutional Selectivity* 50

Table 7.7 *Respondents' Primary Seminar Type Across All Institutions* 51

Table 7.8 *Percentage of Respondents Reporting Primary Seminar Type by Institutional Affiliation* 51

Table 7.9 *Percentage of Respondents Reporting Primary Seminar Type by Institutional Type* 52

Table 7.10 *Percentage of Respondents Reporting Approximate Class Size Across All Institutions* 52

Table 7.11 *Percentage of Respondents Reporting Approximate Class Size by Institutional Affiliation*..53

Table 7.12 *Percentage of Respondents Reporting Approximate Class Size by Institutional Selectivity*..53

Table 7.13 *Percentage of First-Year Students Required to Take Seminar Across All Institutions*..54

Table 7.14 *Percentage of First-Year Students Required to Take Seminar by Institutional Affiliation*..54

Table 7.15 *Type of Students Required to Take Seminar Across All Institutions*...55

Table 7.16 *Type of Students Required to Take Seminar by Institutional Selectivity*..55

Table 7.17 *Percentage of Special Sections Offered Across All Institutions*...........56

Table 7.18 *Percentage of Special Sections Offered by Institutional Affiliation*.....57

Table 7.19 *Percentage of Special Sections Offered by Institutional Enrollment*...58

Table 7.20 *Percentage of Special Sections Offered by Institutional Selectivity*.....59

Table 7.21 *Teaching Responsibility Across All Institutions*................................60

Table 7.22 *Teaching Responsibility by Institutional Affiliation*.........................60

Table 7.23 *Teaching Responsibility by Institutional Selectivity*.........................61

Table 7.24 *Percentage of Institutions Reporting Team-Taught Sections Across All Institutions*..61

Table 7.25 *Percentage of Students Enrolled in Team-Taught Sections Across All Institutions*..62

Table 7.26 *Percentage of Students Team Taught by Institutional Affiliation*........62

Table 7.27 *Team Teaching by Seminar Type*..62

Table 7.28 *Institutions with Sections Taught by Academic Advisor Across All Institutions*..63

Table 7.29 *Institutions with Sections Taught by Academic Advisor by Institutional Affiliation*..63

Table 7.30 *Institutions with Sections Taught by Academic Advisor by Institutional Selectivity*..63

Table 7.31 *Percentage of Students Enrolled in Sections Taught by Academic Advisors Across All Institutions*..................................64

Table 7.32 *Percentage of Students Enrolled in Sections Taught by Academic Advisor by Institutional Affiliation*..................................64

Table 7.33 *Faculty Workload Configuration Across All Institutions*..................65

Table 7.34 *Faculty Workload Configuration by Institutional Selectivity*..............65

Table 7.35 *Faculty Workload Configuration by Seminar Type*.........................65

Table 7.36 *Administrative Staff Workload Configuration Across All Institutions*..66

Table 7.37 *Administrative Staff Workload Configuration by Enrollment*............66

Table 7.38 *Administrative Staff Workload Configuration by Institutional Selectivity*..66

Table 7.39 *Instructor Compensation Across All Institutions*.............................67

Table 7.40 *Instructor Compensation by Institutional Affiliation*..................67
Table 7.41 *Instructor Training Offered Across All Institutions*..........................68
Table 7.42 *Instructor Training Offered by Seminar Type*..........................68
Table 7.43 *Instructor Training Required Across All Institutions*........................68
Table 7.44 *Instructor Training Required by Institutional Selectivity*................68
Table 7.45 *Length of Instructor Training Across All Institutions*......................69
Table 7.46 *Percentage of Seminars That Carry Credit Toward Graduation*
          Across All Institutions...69
Table 7.47 *Percentage of Seminars That Carry Credit Toward Graduation*
          by Institutional Selectivity...70
Table 7.48 *Application of Credit Across All Institutions*.................................70
Table 7.49 *Application of Credit by Institutional Affiliation*..........................70
Table 7.50 *Application of Credit by Institutional Selectivity*...........................71
Table 7.51 *Credit Hours Offered Across All Institutions*................................71
Table 7.52 *Credit Hours Offered by Institutional Selectivity*..........................72
Table 7.53 *Credit Hours Offered by Seminar Type*......................................72
Table 7.54 *Method of Grading Across All Institutions*.................................73
Table 7.55 *Seminar Length Across All Institutions*.....................................73
Table 7.56 *Contact Hours Per Week Across All Institutions*............................74
Table 7.57 *Contact Hours by Institutional Selectivity*....................................74
Table 7.58 *Contact Hours Per Week by Seminar Type*..................................75
Table 7.59 *Seminar Includes Service-Learning Component Across All*
          Institutions..75
Table 7.60 *Seminar Includes Service-Learning Component by Institutional*
          Affiliation...76
Table 7.61 *Seminar Includes Service-Learning Component by Institutional*
          Enrollment..76
Table 7.62 *Seminar Includes Service-Learning Component by Seminar Type*......76
Table 7.63 *Seminar is Part of Learning Community Across All Institutions*.......76
Table 7.64 *Seminar is Part of Learning Community by Institutional*
          Affiliation...77
Table 7.65 *Seminar is Part of Learning Community by Institutional*
          Enrollment..77
Table 7.66 *Administrative Home of First-Year Seminar Across All*
          Institutions..78
Table 7.67 *Administrative Home of First-Year Seminar by Institutional*
          Affiliation...78
Table 7.68 *Administrative Home of First-Year Seminar by Institutional*
          Enrollment..79
Table 7.69 *Administrative Home of First-Year Seminar by Seminar Type*..........79
Table 7.70 *Seminar Has Director/Coordinator Across All Institutions*..............79
Table 7.71 *Seminar Has Director/Coordinator by Institutional Affiliation*..........80
Table 7.72 *Seminar Has Director/Coordinator by Institutional Enrollment*........80

Table 7.73 *Seminar Has Director/Coordinator by Seminar Type* 80

Table 7.74 *Status of Director/Coordinator Across All Institutions* 80

Table 7.75 *Status of Director/Coordinator by Institutional Affiliation* 81

Table 7.76 *Status of Director/Coordinator by Seminar Type* 81

Table 7.77 *Other Role of Director/Coordinator Across All Institutions* 81

Table 7.78 *Most Important Course Objectives Across All Institutions* 82

Table 7.79 *Most Important Course Objectives by Institutional Affiliation* 83

Table 7.80 *Most Important Course Objectives by Institutional Selectivity* 84

Table 7.81 *Most Important Course Objectives by Seminar Type* 85

Table 7.82 *Most Important Course Topics Across All Institutions* 86

Table 7.83 *Most Important Course Topics by Institutional Affiliation* 87

Table 7.84 *Most Important Course Topics by Institutional Selectivity* 88

Table 7.85 *Most Important Seminar Topics by Seminar Type* 89

Table 7.86 *Results Attributed to First-Year Seminars Across All Institutions* 90

Table 7.87 *Results Attributed to First-Year Seminars by Institutional Affiliation* 91

Table 7.88 *Results Attributed to First-Year Seminar by Seminar Type* 92

Table 8.1 *Comparison of Institutions Offering First-Year Seminar, 1988-2003* 95

Table 8.2 *Comparison of Survey Results, 1988-2003* 96

Foreword

Betsy O. Barefoot

In the summer of 1988 when I began working as a graduate assistant at the National Resource Center for The "Freshman" Year Experience, the Center was receiving responses to the first national survey of freshman seminars. By reviewing these survey responses, I acquired my first introduction to the "freshman seminar." As I continued my work at the National Center, the freshman or, first-year, seminar became the area of focus for my doctoral dissertation, which was based on the results of the 1991 National Survey of Freshman Seminar Programs. While developing a national database of information on this now ubiquitous course type was important, my most meaningful knowledge about first-year seminars resulted from personal experience over several years of teaching University 101 at the University of South Carolina. Through that teaching experience, I learned about the power of the first-year seminar as a device for connecting students to a particular campus and to collegiate life in general. I also learned about the difficulty of teaching a course in which the primary focus is the student. My best-laid plans often did not work out, and student needs frequently took the class discussion in different directions. Moreover, my responsibilities as an instructor extended well beyond "contact hours."

In the early 1990s, the future of the first-year seminar in American higher education was uncertain. In my 1992 dissertation, I remarked: "No one can accurately predict whether or to what degree the current popularity of the freshman seminar will continue or how this course will evolve over time" (Barefoot, p. 147). But in the intervening 12 years, seminars have not vanished; rather, their numbers continue to increase, and they remain some of the most innovative and flexible courses in the college curriculum. Research continues to link these courses with improved retention and graduation rates, and, in some cases, improved academic performance for participants. And as this monograph reports, seminars are moving into the 21st century through the significant integration of technology and through connection with other important curricular components and structures such as service-learning and learning communities.

In spite of their utility and documented successes, many seminars continue to face an ongoing struggle for credibility. This struggle is often played out in decisions about credit and contact hours. A disturbing percentage of seminar courses continue to carry one hour of credit or 14 contact hours over the course of a semester. While I could argue that 14 hours is better than nothing, it is unreasonable to expect maximum impact from a minimal experience. Other struggles relate to the awarding of academic credit for what is often perceived to be "fluff" or content students "should have known before coming to college." Just as the first college year often becomes a campus lightning rod for differences of opinion about the overall purpose of higher education, so the first-year seminar becomes the lightning rod for discussions and debates about what topics and processes are worthy of college-level credit.

Readers should understand that these descriptive findings are not necessarily recommendations. Decisions about credit, contact hours, instructional responsibility, and content are best made by each campus in context of student characteristics, institutional mission, and the purpose the seminar is intended to achieve. Careful assessment of the first-year seminar is the only way for institutions to know if these decisions were effective in achieving course goals.

As someone who has followed the growth of first-year seminars as both a scholar and an instructor, I commend this monograph as a must-read for educators who are interested in the first year. Barbara Tobolowsky and her colleagues at the National Resource Center have done a marvelous job designing the survey, on which this monograph is based, in a way that allows us to capture new information about the structure and delivery of these courses. Moreover, her analysis is reported in a way that I believe will help readers place their seminar in a national context and will be a catalyst for the creation and re-creation of viable seminars for successive cohorts of first-year students.

Betsy O. Barefoot
Co-Director and Senior Scholar
Policy Center on the First Year of College
Brevard, NC

Reference

Barefoot, B. O. (1992). *Helping first-year college students climb the academic ladder: Report of a national survey of freshman seminar programming in American higher education.* Unpublished doctoral dissertation, College of William and Mary, Williamsburg, VA.

Introduction

Barbara F. Tobolowsky

In 1988, the National Resource Center for The Freshman Year Experience conducted the first National Survey on Freshman Seminar Programs. Published in 1991, the resulting monograph was the first known attempt to provide a national, empirical snapshot of the first-year seminar. This survey instrument focused on investigating the characteristics of seminars, but there was no standard way of describing the different types of seminars on American campuses. As part of her dissertation research, Betsy Barefoot (1992) analyzed approximately 200 course descriptions and other related materials to create a typology of five distinct seminar types. The 1991 survey used this typology to determine, with some precision, how many of each type of seminar existed on the survey participants' campuses. Even then, hybrids existed. In fact, the monograph reporting the findings from the 1991 survey noted that approximately 30% of the seminars offered were some combination of two or more types (Barefoot & Fidler, 1992). Still, the typology helped us better understand the commonalities and differences of first-year seminars. By 1994, the National Resource Center had undergone a name change, now known as the National Resource Center for The Freshman Year Experience and Students in Transition, and the survey was fine-tuned again to garner more information on the administrative structure of the seminar.

Since 1994, the survey has continued to be administered every three years with slight changes, but with many different stewards at its helm. Now, it is my turn. In 2002, I joined the staff of the (now-called) National Resource Center for The First-Year Experience and Students in Transition, and one of my first goals was to revise the seminar survey. Initially, my plans were just to reorganize it. As I began to work through the survey and make changes to the order and, in some cases, the wording of questions, I sought feedback from Mary Stuart Hunter, John Gardner, Betsy Barefoot, and others. Stuart thought it was time to join the 21st century and offer a web-based survey rather than the standard hard-copy version. John recommended that I explore new areas, such as online courses, and go in greater depth in others (e.g., learning communities, instructor compensation). Betsy challenged me to go back to the beginning and revisit each question on the previous survey and consider if it was still appropriate at this point in the history of first-year seminars. All the comments reflected how the times and the seminar had changed and how the survey needed to capture those changes.

With the gauntlet thrown, Carrie Linder, the Center's resources and research coordinator at the time, Marla Mamrick, our graduate assistant, and I sat down and spent considerable time going through the survey and determining which questions should stay, which should go, which needed to be rewritten, and which needed to be added. These efforts resulted in countless drafts. Along the way, we conducted a pilot of the new instrument with faculty and staff from around the country. Their valuable comments led to more revisions. As a result of these efforts, a new instrument was born.

The 2003 National Survey on First-Year Seminars is the first time since 1991 that the survey has gone through such a major overhaul. I had no idea when I started my reorganization project in 2002 that we would end up creating a new instrument. However, thanks to the hard work of Carrie, Marla, Mey Wu (our web master), Kerry Mitchell (our survey guru), and others, we were able to administer the survey in fall 2003, right on schedule.

Just as the survey changed, we are reporting the results in a different way as well. In chapter 1, Marla Mamrick offers a brief history of first-year seminars and an overview of findings from previous survey administrations to provide some context for the 2003 results. Chapter 2 describes the methodology employed in this administration. In the next three chapters, we focus on a few areas we found particularly interesting. In chapter 3, the primary differences between seminars in two-year and four-year institutions are explored. Chapter 4 relates information gleaned regarding teaching the seminar, including team-teaching configurations, compensation, and innovative pedagogical approaches. Then, in chapter 5, a focused report of the assessment efforts conducted on participants' campuses is offered. Chapter 6 explores seminar elements that have made an impact on the course, from delivery changes (i.e., seminars with online elements to seminars embedded in learning communities) to course components (i.e., service-learning). Chapter 7 presents more than 80 tables that reflect the full portrait of the first-year seminar that emerged from the survey. The final chapter provides a brief summary of key findings and seminar trends across all survey iterations. The appendices include the new instrument, the names of participating institutions, and a brief description of first-year seminars as described by the proprietary institutions that participated in this survey administration. This was the first time that for-profit institutions were included in data collection. Though the response rate makes it impossible for us to make any general comments about seminars in this unique sector, we were eager to share the anecdotal information that emerged.

Creating the survey, analyzing the data, and producing this monograph took the time and energy of many people. Thanks go to Phil Moore, director of institutional planning and assessment at the University of South Carolina, who ran all the statistics so we could analyze the data and make sense of it all; Brad Cox, the current coordinator of research and public information, for his assistance in the analysis and creation of tables; and Tracy Skipper, our editorial projects coordinator, and the publication graduate assistants for their work in preparing the manuscript. I also would like to thank Stuart, Betsy, Carrie, Marla, Phil, and Jennifer Keup (director of follow-up surveys at the Higher Education Research Institute at UCLA) for providing feedback on the monograph. Finally, I would like to thank all the responding institutions (see Appendix B for the names of participating institutions). Our survey is only useful if there are participants willing to take the time to complete it. Thanks to you all.

We learned a great deal in the process of creating and administering the survey and analyzing the findings. We hope we have been able to paint for readers a clear picture of first-year seminars on participating college campuses in fall 2003. We further hope that the findings reported here provide educators greater insight into first-year seminars and that they can use this information on their own campuses to improve the first-year seminar, thereby supporting first-year students—the ultimate goal of all such courses.

Barbara F. Tobolowsky
Associate Director
National Resource Center for The First-Year Experience and
Students in Transition
University of South Carolina
Columbia, SC

References

Barefoot, B. O. (1992). *Helping first-year college students climb the academic ladder: Report of a national survey of freshman seminar programming in American higher education.* Unpublished doctoral dissertation, College of William and Mary, Willamsburg, VA.

Barefoot, B. O., & Fidler, P. P. (1992). *The 1991 national survey of freshman seminar programming: Helping first-year college students climb the academic ladder* (Monograph No. 10). Columbia, SC: University of South Carolina, National Resource Center for The Freshman Year Experience.

The First-Year Seminar: An Historical Perspective

Marla Mamrick

1

In the late 1880s, Boston University introduced the first seminar designed to orient its first-year students to the campus (Gordon, 1989). Over the next few decades, a number of institutions followed its lead and offered first-year seminars. The development of the seminar received an additional boost with the 1913 Gott v. Berea decision, "which articulated the concept of *in loco parentis*" (Gahagan, 2002, p. 5). Gahagan notes that this ruling gave "educators…the specific responsibility for the care and welfare of their students" (p. 5). One aspect of that care was assisting students in their college transition, and the first-year seminar proved to be an ideal means of helping institutions function in this way. By 1930, approximately one third of the colleges and universities offered first-year seminars (Gordon).

However, by the end of the turbulent 1960s, colleges were no longer assuming the parental role with students and that, along with other campus changes, led to the discontinuation of many first-year seminars designed to help students adjust to college life. Dwyer (1989) reports three changes that encouraged campuses to reinstate the first-year seminar in the 1970s. First, educators recognized that students were not getting sufficient help from informal networks (i.e., peers). Second, campuses were opening their doors to more and more students, many of whom were underprepared for the rigors of higher education and needed more formal supports to succeed. Third, curricular requirements and institutional policies became more and more complicated, so students needed assistance to decipher the information. These circumstances led to the grass-roots movement led by John Gardner and others to reintroduce the first-year seminar on American college campuses.

By the 1980s, the first-year seminar was once again playing an important role in American higher education. The National Resource Center for The Freshman Year Experience conducted the first National Survey of Freshman Seminar Programs in 1988 to better understand the phenomenon. The Center continues to administer the survey triennially in order to offer a rich portrait of the ever-evolving first-year seminar.

Despite the changes to the survey over the years, the purpose of the survey has remained the same throughout each administration: to provide an understanding of the types and characteristics of first-year seminars offered on college and university campuses throughout the United States. With 15 years of historical data on first-year seminars, trends in course description, content, and administration become apparent. A summary of previous findings follows.

Types of First-Year Seminars

The 1991 survey (Barefoot & Fidler, 1992) provided definitions for the most common types of seminars. The definitions for these types have changed very little since they were originally introduced by Barefoot (1992). Although some institutions offer hybrids or variations on these seminars, the following five types continue to be the most prevalent on today's campuses:

1. *Extended Orientation Seminar.* Sometimes called a freshman orientation, college survival, college transition, or student success course. Content likely will include introduction to campus resources, time management, academic and career planning, learning strategies, and an introduction to student development issues.
2. *Academic seminar with generally uniform academic content across sections.* May be an interdisciplinary or theme-oriented course, sometimes part of a general education requirement. Primary focus is on academic theme/discipline but will often include academic skills components such as critical thinking and expository writing.
3. *Academic seminars on various topics.* Similar to previously mentioned academic seminar except that specific topics vary from section to section.
4. *Pre-professional or discipline-linked seminar.* Designed to prepare students for the demands of the major/discipline and the profession. Generally taught within professional schools or specific disciplines.
5. *Basic study skills seminar.* Offered for academically underprepared students. The focus is on basic academic skills such as grammar, note taking, and reading texts.

Summary of Past Survey Results

The information highlighted in this chapter includes data from the following survey years: 1988, 1991, 1994, 1997, and 2000 (Barefoot & Fidler, 1992, 1996; Fidler & Fidler, 1991; National Resource Center, 2002).[1] By looking more closely at these earlier survey findings, the current results are put into context. It should be stated that although many of the same institutions participated in multiple administrations, some variation exists among participants throughout the years. Therefore, the results do not track specific changes at institutions; rather, they represent trends that have developed over the years.

Course Description

Since 1988, approximately 70% of institutions responding to the survey indicated that their institutions offer first-year seminars. Extended orientation seminars have continued to be the most common type of seminar offered by

16

survey participants. However, the number of survey participants offering academic seminars has increased (by approximately five percentage points) and basic study skills seminars have decreased (from a high of 6% in 1991 to a low of 3.6% in 2000) throughout this period.

Regardless of seminar type, the maximum number of students enrolled in a section has varied over the years, especially by institutional size and type (i.e., two-year and four-year institutions). Even though variations in class size exist, it is apparent that smaller seminar sections, with 25 or fewer students, have been favored over larger seminar sections.

The number of institutions that reported the seminar course was letter-graded increased dramatically from 62% of reporting institutions in 1988 to 82% in 2000. Similarly, an 8% increase in the number of respondents who indicated their institution offered academic credit for their seminar occurred over this time span. In 2000, 90% of responding institutions reported offering academic credit for their first-year seminar. Bearing in mind that most institutions offer academic credit for the seminar course, respondents most frequently indicated that credit is applied as an elective. However, through the years, almost half of the respondents noted that seminar credits were applied toward either general education or core requirements. In addition, since 1988 about half of the institutions have reported that their seminar is required of all first-year students.

Course Content

The top three reported goals for the seminar have remained the same over the past four survey administrations: (a) develop essential academic skills, (b) provide orientation to campus, and (c) ease transition to campus. Likewise, the top three reported course topics have remained relatively consistent across each of the administrations. The topics reported most frequently include: (a) academic skills (all years), (b) time management (all years), and (c) introduction to campus resources (all but 2000).

In 1994, a question was added to the survey to determine the extent to which institutions link the first-year seminar to one or more other courses (i.e., learning community). Some variation exists in the percentage of institutions reporting such linkages throughout the years from 17.2% in 1994 to 25.1% in 2000.

Course Instruction

Historically, a variety of campus personnel have served as seminar instructors. Since 1991, a gradual increase in the percentage of faculty members providing seminar instruction has been reported. Faculty has remained the most frequently reported group responsible for first-year seminar instruction, followed by student affairs professionals. Other campus staff members such as coaches, academic administrators, librarians, and chaplains have been reported to provide seminar instruction as well. Additionally, the use of undergraduate students as seminar instructors has increased slightly since 1991.

Since 1991, institutions have reported that first-year seminars tend to be part of faculty's regular teaching load rather than an overload. Conversely, teaching has been reported more often as an additional responsibility rather than as part of their regular work for administrators.

Over all the previous survey iterations, nearly three quarters of the institutions have indicated that they offer training for instructors, and almost half of the institutions require training for instructors.

Conclusion

Although there has been some variation in terms of which institutions participated in each survey administration, it is telling that the results have been fairly consistent. This brief overview of key findings reflects a stable trend regarding the administration and execution of first-year seminars even though the instrument itself has undergone changes with each administration. (A complete table including 2003 data representing the continuation of these trends is available in chapter 8.) We offer this brief overview of the history of the survey findings to help you put the most recent results in context.

Notes

[1]All survey iterations were conducted similarly with whole populations, not random samples. Surveys were mailed to chief academic officers of only regionally accredited two- and four-year institutions.

References

Barefoot, B. O. (1992). *Helping first-year college students climb the academic ladder: Report of a national survey of freshman seminar programming in American higher education.* Unpublished doctoral dissertation, College of William and Mary, Williamsburg, VA.

Barefoot, B. O., & Fidler, P. P. (1992). *The 1991 national survey of freshman seminar programming: Helping first-year college students climb the academic ladder* (Monograph No. 10). Columbia, SC: University of South Carolina, National Resource Center for The Freshman Year Experience.

Barefoot, B. O., & Fidler, P. P. (1996). *The 1994 national survey of freshman seminar programs: Continuing innovations in the collegiate curriculum* (Monograph No. 20). Columbia, SC: University of South Carolina, National Resource Center for The Freshman Year Experience and Students in Transition.

Dwyer, J. O. (1989). A historical look at the freshman year experience. In M. L.

Upcraft & J. N. Gardner (Eds.), *The freshman year experience* (pp. 24-39). San Francisco: Jossey-Bass.

Fidler, P. P., & Fidler, D. S. (1991). *First national survey on freshman seminar programs: Findings, conclusions, and recommendations* (Monograph No. 6). Columbia, SC: University of South Carolina, National Resource Center for The Freshman Year Experience.

Gahagan, J. S. (2002). A historical and theoretical framework for the first-year seminar. In National Resource Center for The First-Year Experience and Students in Transition, *The 2000 national survey of first-year seminar programs: Continuing innovations in the collegiate curriculum* (Monograph No. 35) (pp. 5-10). Columbia, SC: University of South Carolina, National Resource Center for The First-Year Experience and Students in Transition.

Gordon, V. N. (1989). Origins and purposes of the freshman seminar. In M. L. Upcraft & J. N. Gardner (Eds.), *The freshman year experience* (pp. 183-197). San Francisco: Jossey-Bass.

National Resource Center for The First-Year Experience and Students in Transition. (2002). *The 2002 national survey of first-year seminar programs: Continuing innovations in the collegiate curriculum* (Monograph No. 35). Columbia, SC: University of South Carolina, Author.

Survey Methodology

2

The 2003 National Survey on First-Year Seminars underwent significant revision from previous survey instruments. In May and early June 2003, a pilot study was conducted to test the clarity and readability of new and revised questions, and feedback from the pilot study was incorporated into the final instrument. The extended length of the revised survey, as well as a desire to reduce administrative costs, figured into the decision to move from a paper-based survey to an electronic version, so the pilot was conducted via e-mail. Feedback from the pilot led to further survey revisions and prompted the decision to offer the survey via the web rather than e-mail. Anecdotally, several people were consulted who had conducted web-based surveys with some success. Their testimony supported our decision.

In October 2003, the National Resource Center sent an e-mail invitation to participate in the web-based 2003 seminar survey to the chief academic officer or the chief executive officer, if the chief academic officer position was vacant, at all regionally accredited higher education institutions identified as having undergraduate students and lower-division courses on their campus. The sample ($N = 3,258$) was drawn from the *2003 Higher Education Directory* (Burke). Not all e-mail invitations were deliverable; 384 invitation e-mails were returned. Also, some additional institutions were without an active or published e-mail address for the chief academic officer or chief executive officer. These two groups were mailed a letter directing them to the survey web site. In all, letters were mailed to 511 institutions. A follow-up e-mail message was sent in mid-November to institutional representatives with e-mail addresses who had not yet completed the survey. Survey responses were collected through November 24, 2003.

In total, survey responses were obtained from 771 institutions for an overall response rate of 23.7%. The respondents included 629 institutions offering a seminar and 142 institutions not offering a first-year seminar. Chi-square analyses were conducted by type of seminar, type of institution (public/private, two-year/four-year), institution size, and selectivity.

Table 2.1 reveals a modest over-representation of public and private four-year institutions and an under-representation of proprietary institutions but a representative sample of two-year institutions in the response population.

The response rate is the primary limitation to this survey. Solomon (2001) notes that web-based surveys have significantly lower response rates than paper surveys. He also emphasizes the value of hyperlinks to the survey to ease survey access. Both the e-mail invitations and letters gave the web address, but the e-mails did not provide a hyperlink to the survey itself. Therefore, the survey was not as easily accessible as it might have been. Future iterations will address this issue.

Table 2.1

Representation of 2003 Survey Respondents Compared to National Average by Institutional Type and Size (N = 771)

Type of institution	Number of institutions responding to survey	Percentage	National percentage by type
Public four-year	176	22.8**	15.0
5,000 or less	59		
5,001 - 10,000	48		
10,001 - 15,000	23		
15,001 - 20,000	25		
More than 20,000	21		
Private four-year	345	44.7**	36.7
5,000 or less	318		
5,001 - 10,000	18		
10,001 - 15,000	6		
15,001 - 20,000	0		
More than 20,000	1		
Two-year	229	29.7	29.1
Proprietary	21	2.7**	19.3

Note. Two private institutions did not include information regarding their size, so they are included in the composite but not the disaggregated categories by size. The national averages come from the *2003 Chronicle Almanac* retrieved June 9, 2004, from http://chronicle.com/free/almanac/2003/nation/nation.htm
**$p < .01$

Nevertheless, this survey administration offers data from more than 600 institutions that offer first-year seminars, providing the most complete portrait of seminar structure and administration that is currently available. All reported percentages are based on those institutions that offer first-year seminars. Thus, although the response rate and the institutional representation are not optimal, with the necessary cautions employed, readers can gather information that will help them develop, improve, and understand their own first-year seminars.

References

Burke, J. M. (Ed.). (2003). *2003 higher education directory*. Falls Church, VA: Higher Education Publications.

Solomon, D. J. (2001). Conducting web-based surveys. *Practical Assessment, Research & Evaluation*. Retrieved October 20, 2004, from http://PAREonline.net/getvn.asp?v=7&n=19

A Two-Year and Four-Year Institutional Comparison

3

This chapter provides a portrait of first-year seminars at two- and four-year institutions[1]. In addition, a comparison between institutional types is included in the text allowing readers a chance to compare their college or university to similar and different institutional types.

General Profile of Reporting Institutions

In this section, basic information regarding institutional profile, control, and size of participating institutions is reported.

Two-Year Institutions

Approximately one quarter (26.3%) of the survey respondents represented two-year institutions. Most of the two-year institutions were public (88.9%) and on the semester system (94.3%). As reported in Table 3.1, these institutions tended to have 5,000 or fewer undergraduate students (62%).

Table 3.1
Undergraduate Headcount at Two-Year Institutions (n = 163)

Size of student body	Number of institutions	Percentage
5,000 or less	101	62.0
5,001 - 10,000	30	18.4
10,001 - 15,000	15	9.2
15,001 - 20,000	8	5.0
More than 20,000	9	5.5

Four-Year Institutions

The majority of reporting institutions were from the four-year sector (73.8%), and the majority of those were private institutions (64.6%) on the semester system (93.7%). Just as was the case for the two-year institutions, most of the four-year institutions have 5,000 or fewer undergraduate students (71.4%) (see Table 3.2).

Table 3.2
Undergraduate Headcount at Four-Year Institutions (n = 458)

Size of student body	Number of institutions	Percentage
5,000 or less	327	71.4
5,001 - 10,000	58	12.7
10,001 - 15,000	28	6.1
15,001 - 20,000	24	5.2
More than 20,000	21	4.6

The First-Year Seminar – Longevity and Participation

This section reports how long the seminars have been in existence, how many students take the seminars, and what type of seminars are found on the campuses of responding institutions.

Two-Year Institutions

Among two-year institutions that responded to the survey, most have offered their first-year seminar for more than two years (88.7%), with only 11.3% offering the seminar for two years or less, and one third of the institutions having offered it for more than 10 years. Student participation in the seminar varied. Almost one third of the reporting institutions responded that 76% to 100% of their students participated in a seminar, and 40.5% of the reporting institutions had fewer than 25% of their students enrolled in a seminar (see Table 3.3).

Table 3.3
Percentage of First-Year Students who Take the Seminar at Two-Year Institutions (n = 153)

Percentage of first-year students who take the seminar	Number of institutions	Percentage
Less than 25%	62	40.5
25 - 50%	21	13.7
51 - 75%	22	14.4
76 - 100%	48	31.4

Institutions were asked to report every type of first-year seminar that they offered on their campuses. As reflected in Table 3.4, most two-year institutions offered extended orientation seminars (79.8%), with just over a third offering basic study skills seminars (37.4%). Seminars with academic content (i.e., both variable and uniform content) were seldom offered at the two-year institutions responding to the survey.

Table 3.4
Type of First-Year Seminars at Two-Year Institutions (n = 163)

Type of seminar	Number of institutions	Percentage
Extended orientation	130	79.8
Academic seminar with uniform content	30	18.4
Academic seminar with variable content	12	7.4
Pre-professional seminar	17	10.4
Basic study skills	61	37.4
Other	9	5.5

Note. Percentages do not equal 100%. Institutions could select more than one type of seminar.

Four-Year Institutions

Just as was the case with the reporting two-year institutions, most of the participating four-year institutions have offered first-year seminars for more than two years. Only 7.8% of the schools have offered them for less than two years, with 43.9% having offered them for more than 10 years.

A far larger percentage of first-year students on four-year campuses participated in the seminars than on the two-year campuses, with 69.5% of the four-year institutions reporting that between 76% and 100% of their first-year students took the seminar (see Table 3.5).

Table 3.5
Percentage of First-Year Students who Take the Seminar at Four-Year Institutions (n = 449)

Percentage of first-year students who take the seminar	Number of institutions	Percentage
Less than 25%	48	10.7
25 - 50%	49	10.9
51 - 75%	40	8.9
76 - 100%	312	69.5

The most commonly reported type of seminar on four-year campuses was the extended orientation seminar (Table 3.6) as was the case at two-year

Table 3.6

Type of First-Year Seminars at Four-Year Institutions (n = 458)

Type of seminar	Number of institutions	Percentage
Extended orientation	275	60.0
Academic seminar with uniform content	140	30.6
Academic seminar with variable content	139	30.4
Pre-professional seminar	71	15.5
Basic study skills	63	13.8
Other	42	9.2

Note. Percentages do not equal 100%. Institutions could select more than one type of seminar.

institutions. In fact, 43.4% of four-year and 69.7% of two-year institutions selected this type of seminar as having the highest total student enrollment of all seminar types offered on their campuses. Whereas the basic study skills seminar was the second most commonly reported seminar type among two-year institutions, academic seminars with variable or uniform content were much more likely to be offered on the four-year campuses.

A small percentage of four-year (9.2%) and two-year institutions (5.5%) reported offering some "other" type of seminar. These courses generally were hybrids combining one or more of the primary types of seminars. There were some exceptions. For example, one four-year institution offered "College Life," which emphasized the "integration of faith and learning," and another four-year institution reported having a wilderness orientation as its first-year seminar.

The Students

This section reports information provided by survey participants regarding the students who take the more prevalent type of seminar on individual campuses. In most instances, but not all, that seminar was an extended orientation seminar. For more specific data by seminar type, see chapter 7.

Two-Year Institutions

Seminar sections tended to be relatively small at participating institutions. At the 159 two-year campuses in this study, 43.2% of the sections had between 21 and 25 students, and 29.7% had 16 to 20 students. The seminars were required of all students at 22% of the participating two-year institutions; however, on almost a third of the campuses, no students were required to take the seminar (see Table 3.7).

Table 3.7
Percentage of Two-Year Institutions That Require First-Year Seminars (n = 159)

Percentage of students required to take seminar	Number of institutions	Percentage
100%	35	22.0
90 - 99%	12	7.6
80 - 89%	11	6.9
70 - 79%	10	6.3
60 - 69%	7	4.4
50 - 59%	1	0.6
Less than 50%	34	21.4
0%	49	30.8

The seminar was rarely required of a specific group of students at reporting two-year institutions. When it was required, it was more frequently required for provisionally admitted students (11.7%), students in specific majors (8.6%), undeclared students (7.8%), athletes (6.3%), learning community participants (5.5%), and honors students (3.1%). Almost half of the institutions reported that no special sections were offered. However, on some campuses, special sections were offered, but not required, for academically underprepared students (25.8%), learning community participants (13.5%), students within certain majors (10.4%), international students (4.3%), honors students (3.7%), undeclared students (3.1%), pre-professional students (2.5%), and transfer students (2.5%).

Four-Year Institutions

At four-year institutions, most class sections enrolled fewer than 25 students. In fact, 20.4% of the classes enrolled between 10 and 15 students (only 8% of the two-year institutions had classes this small); 38.4% had 16 to 20 students in each class (almost 30% of the two-year campuses reported classes this size), and 30.3% of the sections had between 21 and 25 students in a class (the most common class size at two-year institutions at 43.2%). Many more four-year campuses reported requiring the seminar of all their first-year students (55.5% vs. 22% at two-year campuses), and fewer of them had completely voluntary enrollment (16% of four-years vs. 30.8% of two-years) (see Table 3.8).

When the seminar was required for specific subgroups of students at reporting four-year institutions, they were most likely to be the following: (a) provisionally admitted students (26.3%), (b) learning community participants (17.1%), (c) student athletes (13.2%), (d) undeclared students (13.2%), (e) honors students (11.2%), and (f) students in specific majors (6.8%). Institutions also

Table 3.8
Percentage of Four-Year Institutions That Require First-Year Seminars (n = 456)

Percentage of students required to take first-year seminars	Number of institutions	Percentage
100%	253	55.5
90 - 99%	41	9.0
80 - 89%	6	1.3
70 - 79%	11	2.4
60 - 69%	9	2.0
50 - 59%	4	0.9
Less than 50%	59	12.9
0%	73	16.0

reported offering, but not requiring, participation in special sections for honors students (23.4%), academically underprepared students (18.8%), students within a specific major (16.4%), learning community participants (15.9%), undeclared students (9.2%), pre-professional students (8.3%), students residing within a particular residence hall (6.8%), transfer students (6.6%), and international students (5.2%).

The Instructors

Focusing on some new areas related to instruction, the 2003 survey explored who taught the course, the prevalence of team-teaching, details regarding team configurations, and compensation. See chapter 4 for those results. The survey also explored specifics regarding instructor training. Those results follow.

Two-Year Institutions

First-year seminar instructor training was offered at 55.6% of the two-year institutions participating in the survey. Of those institutions offering training, almost one half of them offered a half day or less of instructor training (48.3%), with two-day training being the second most reported time frame (16.9%). In addition, most instructors were required to participate in training (72.7%) when it was available.

Four-Year Institutions

Four-year campuses participating in the survey were far more likely to report offering instructor training (78.3%). Of those campuses offering training,

33% provide a half day or less of training, almost a quarter provide a one-day training (24.6%), and 18.1% offered a two-day training. A small percentage of reporting institutions offered training for a longer time frame than two days (e.g., 5.4% of reporting institutions offered three days of training, 2.5% offered four days of training, and 2.8% offered one week of training). Of those institutions that offered training, 67.8% required their first-year instructors to attend.

The Course

The specific characteristics associated with the course itself (i.e., course length, credit, objectives, and goals) are reported in this section. (See chapter 7 for aggregated information.) For both two- and four-year institutions, the seminar was typically offered for one term (semester or quarter) (82.2% of two-year institutions and 82.1% of four-year institutions). In a handful of cases, the seminar lasted for a year (5.5% of two-year institutions and 9.4% of four-year institutions).

A few institutions reported less traditional course schedules. For example, several schools offered their seminars for the first six to eight weeks of a semester to front-load information. Others mentioned offering the course intermittently throughout the first semester or first year. One institution provided the seminar in three-week blocks twice a year, and another college mentioned offering the seminar during the special January term. Therefore, though most campuses scheduled the seminar for the fall term, some interesting variations to this pattern were reported.

Two-Year Institutions

At two-year institutions, the seminar counted toward academic credit in 84.1% of reporting schools. Participating institutions most frequently offered letter grades (83.4%) but also offered pass/fail (12.3%) or no grade (4.3%) options. Most often, the course had three contact hours per week (41.1%), with one contact hour being the second most common amount of time reported (31.3%). The amount of credit applied varied from the more common amounts of one credit (55.5%) and three credits (35.8%) to the least common amounts of two credits (13.9%) and five credits (1.5%). The credit generally counted as an elective (59.1%) or towards a general education requirement (36.5%) at the reporting two-year institutions. Curiously, no direct relationship between contact hour and credit was found, but the potential explanation for this inconsistency falls outside the scope of this survey.

Though the predominant type of seminar at the two-year institutions participating in the survey was an extended orientation seminar, respondents reported a range of course objectives and topics. As Table 3.9 reveals, developing academic skills and providing orientation to campus resources were the most commonly mentioned objectives.

Table 3.9
Most Important Course Objectives at Two-Year Institutions (n = 163)

Objective	Number of institutions	Percentage
Develop academic skills	118	72.4
Provide orientation to campus resources	117	71.8
Encourage self-exploration	91	55.8
Develop support network	61	37.4
Increase sophomore return rates	50	30.7
Provide common experience	40	24.5
Increase student/faculty interaction	24	14.7
Introduce a discipline	7	4.3

Note. Institutions were asked to select three responses; therefore, responses equal more than 100%.

The reporting institutions also noted a range of course topics, with study skills, time management, and introducing campus resources being the most commonly noted (see Table 3.10).

Table 3.10
Most Important Course Topics at Two-Year Institutions (n = 163)

Course topics	Number of institutions	Percentage
Study skills	140	85.9
Time management	132	81.0
Campus resources	116	71.2
Academic planning	105	64.4
Career exploration	77	47.2
Critical thinking	73	44.8
College policies	64	39.3
Relationship issues	35	21.5
Diversity issues	34	20.9
Writing skills	29	17.8
Specific disciplinary topic	9	5.5

Note. Institutions were asked to select five responses; therefore, responses equal more than 100%.

Four-Year Institutions

At four-year institutions, 91.2% of the seminars carried academic credit. Most four-year institutions offered letter grades (77.2%) for the seminar but also offered pass/fail (20.8%) or no grade (2%) options. Most often the course had one contact hour (35.4%) or three contact hours (34.3%), but the seminar at some participating four-year institutions (20.7%) had two contact hours. Similarly, the course was more likely to carry one credit (47.5%), with three credits being the next most likely amount (29.6%) reported. The course counted as an elective (36.4%), towards general education (64.1%), or towards the major (6.3%) when credit was applied.

As with the two-year institutions, the reporting four-year institutions were more likely to offer an extended orientation seminar. Consequently, the most important course objectives are similar at two-year and four-year institutions. As Table 3.11 reflects, developing academic skills and providing campus resources were the most important objectives at both types of institutions.

Table 3.11
Most Important Course Objectives at Four-Year Institutions (n = 458)

Objective	Number of institutions	Percentage
Develop academic skills	276	60.3
Provide orientation to campus resources	253	55.2
Encourage self-exploration	156	34.1
Develop support network	169	36.9
Increase sophomore return rates	116	25.3
Provide common experience	184	40.2
Increase student/faculty interaction	170	37.1
Introduce a discipline	38	8.3

Note. Institutions were asked to select three responses; therefore, responses equal more than 100%.

Some interesting differences are seen between the institutional types regarding seminar topics. "Developing academic skills" is the most important objective mentioned at both four-year and two-year institutions. However, "creating a common first-year experience" was mentioned more often at four-year than two-year institutions. The fact that four-year institutions responding to the survey tended to be residential schools and not commuter campuses may account for the difference.

The reporting four-year institutions also noted a range of course topics.

The most common topics (i.e., campus resources, academic planning, study skills, and time management) have been commonly associated with extended orientation seminars in past seminar surveys (See Table 3.12). The only additional topic mentioned significantly more frequently at the four-year institutions than the participating two-year campuses was critical thinking (55% of four-year institutions vs. 44.8% at two-year institutions).

Table 3.12
Most Important Course Topics at Four-Year Institutions (n = 458)

Course topics	Number of institutions	Percentage
Study skills	250	54.6
Time management	239	52.2
Campus resources	266	58.1
Academic planning	256	55.9
Career exploration	140	30.6
Critical thinking	252	55.0
College policies	131	28.6
Relationship issues	133	29.0
Diversity issues	152	33.2
Writing skills	163	35.6
Specific disciplinary topic	116	25.3

Note. Institutions were asked to select five topics; therefore, responses equal more than 100%.

Conclusion

These findings provide a disaggregated portrait by institutional type and offer some comparisons as well. Significantly, the most prevalent type of seminar found in both types of institutions was the extended orientations seminar; therefore, it is not surprising that very little difference was seen between institutions regarding objectives and topics.

Notes

[1]All percentages are based on participating institutions that offer seminars.

Teaching in First-Year Seminars

4

This chapter reports the findings on teaching configurations, workloads and compensation, and innovative teaching methods shared by participating colleges and universities. (For information on instructor training by institutional type, see chapter 3. For other information on training, see chapter 7.)

Teaching Configurations and Workloads

Most two-year and four-year institutions reported that faculty plays a key role in seminar instruction, with 91.1% of four-year institutions and 86.5% of two-year institutions reporting that faculty are responsible for seminar instruction. Instructors at four-year institutions may come from other ranks, such as student affairs professionals (42.8%), undergraduates (8.5%), and graduate students (5.7%). Two-year institutions were much less likely to report that a seminar was taught by graduate (.6%) and undergraduate students (0%) than four-year institutions. However, student affairs professionals played a more significant role as seminar instructors on two-year (52.2%) than on four-year campuses (42.8%). Other people who provided instruction in both sectors included advisors, library staff, and other campus administrators.

Individual instruction existed in most of the institutions participating in this survey, but team teaching was also employed at many four-year and two-year colleges and universities (39.3%). As Table 4.1 reflects, 64 institutions employed teams to teach every one of their first-year seminars. Another 41 institutions reported team teaching in at least one quarter of sections offered. In general, team teaching was more prevalent on four-year campuses (79.7%) than on two-year campuses (20.3%).

Table 4.1
Percentage of First-Year Seminar Sections That Were Team Taught (n = 241)

Percentage of team-taught sections	Number of institutions	Percentage
100%	64	26.6
75 - 99%	9	3.7
50 - 74%	12	5.0
25 - 49%	20	8.3
Less than 25%	136	56.4

Note. Percentages do not equal 100% as multiple responses were given by some participating institutions.

Team teaching can take many forms. Sometimes faculty members were paired with undergraduate or graduate students, other faculty members, or with student or academic affairs professionals (e.g., advising, financial aid, career services). One institution mentioned that male and female faculty taught together, and these teams determined who presented which topics "due to the sensitivity of the issues." In other cases, new faculty members were paired with veteran faculty to teach. At one institution, a senior student was paired with a graduate student or alumnus/a. At other institutions, two student affairs professionals partnered to teach the course.

Sometimes, the team teaching extended beyond just a pair of instructors, and larger teams were formed to handle the teaching duties. Some examples of these configurations included (a) academic faculty, a dean's office advisor, and an advisor from a particular school; (b) faculty, staff, and a student; (c) faculty from three different disciplines; (d) faculty with two students; (e) three administrators; (f) faculty, staff, and library professionals; and (g) faculty, staff, student, and librarian. Clearly, participating campuses adopted many different teaching configurations.

Teaching Load and Compensation

In a majority of cases with faculty as seminar instructors, the seminar was part of their assigned teaching load (68.8%) rather than an overload (39.6%). When administrative staff were seminar instructors, the course was frequently an extra responsibility (58.9%) rather than an assigned responsibility (41.7%) or part of administrative workload (11.3%). In rare cases (9.7% for faculty and 11.3% for administrative staff), the seminar was considered something other than an overload, part of the regular teaching load, an assigned responsibility, or an extra responsibility; and in these instances, the instructors may have volunteered. For staff, the course may have been part of their professional duties or considered part of their institutional service.

The most common form of compensation reported for all instructors was a stipend (74.6%), with fewer than 9% of the institutions reporting that release time was offered as compensation for teaching the seminar. Some institutions tied the stipend to credit hours, instructor experience, and/or faculty rank. Others provided monetary amounts that ranged from $250 to $5,400. The most frequent response was $500, with a mean of approximately $1,250 per section.

Innovative or Successful Course Components

Almost 500 institutions shared elements of their first-year seminar that they deemed innovative or successful. A number of the responding institutions found success using similar approaches. Following are some of the most frequently mentioned innovations grouped by course components, instructors, and pedagogical approaches.

Course Components or Structures

- Integrating the first-year seminar in a learning community
- Integrating the seminar into orientation week activities to front-load information
- Offering online courses or components
- Integrating service-learning into the seminar
- Requiring stand-alone supplemental programs (e.g., lectures, concerts, plays, films) as part of the course
- Offering summer bonding activities such as wilderness camps and common summer reading programs

Instructors

- Using peer leaders
- Providing faculty development, including training prior to teaching and faculty meetings during the term
- Team teaching
- Having advisors teach their advisees

Pedagogical Approaches

- Using reaction or reflection papers in the classroom
- Requiring portfolios

A few methods were mentioned by only a handful of institutions, but these strategies offer some other interesting examples of first-year seminar efforts.

- Faculty at Western Baptist College made home visits to students and their parents in the summer pre-enrollment to discuss class schedules, college housing, and financial aid issues.
- The Queens College–CUNY seminar used active-learning modules in which students "react" to a historical setting.
- Students at Columbus College of Art and Design chose from a menu of sessions according to what is most relevant for them. They had to attend three personal growth sessions, one diversity session, one experiential session, and two mandatory sessions by the end of the semester. In the year prior to reporting, 34 sessions were offered.
- Maryville College discussed having a series of four seminars offered at four points in the school year, i.e., summer orientation, early fall semester, January, and spring semester. Students were required to attend all four sessions.
- Several schools mentioned class trips with first-year students going

to locations such as Jamaica, Belize, and Washington, D.C. (e.g., King College, Lynn University, Northland College, Oregon State University, Rocky Mountain College, and Salisbury University).

- Avila University offered a Friday workshop series that allowed students to go as a group or individually to workshops of their own choosing.
- Castleton State College had an open common hour on Wednesday at noon where students met as a whole or in groups to attend workshops and lectures on various topics (e.g., responsible drinking, wellness, career planning, sex and violence issues, and community service).
- A few schools (e.g., Paul Smith's College) mentioned hosting a class dinner at some point in the semester.
- Bethel College in Kansas discussed assigning roommates to the same advisor, who also taught their first-year seminar. Thus, roommates were in the same seminar section with the same instructor.
- Millersville University used problem-based learning approaches in the classroom.
- Bradley University used games and media as teaching tools (e.g., the use of a Jeopardy-like approach to teaching about campus, students, and resources and the use of an interactive video called *He Said, She Said* to explore gender differences as part of the diversity discussion).
- Some seminar sections enrolled only students from the same residence halls (i.e., Macalester College and Occidental College) and sometimes even the same floors in the residence halls. (e.g., Nazareth College of Rochester)
- Students at Savannah State University created a name for themselves which was reflective of their personalities and characters and used the name throughout the term.

Conclusion

In this chapter, we reported on teaching configurations, compensation, and innovative pedagogical practices. Clearly, many campuses are using innovative strategies in their courses. Hopefully, their ideas will prove inspiring to readers as well. The next chapter focuses exclusively on assessment efforts being conducted on the campuses of responding institutions.

Assessment and the First-Year Seminar

5

In the past survey administrations, only one question explored assessment outcomes. Respondents were asked to select from a list of 12 potential seminar outcomes (including an "Other" option) and submit available research reports with their surveys. In addition to measuring 11 possible survey outcomes (including the "Other" option), the 2003 instrument investigated whether institutions had done any formal program evaluation since fall 2000. Just over half of the respondents (52.4%) marked in the affirmative. The 2003 survey also explored exactly what kinds of assessment were done and which methods were used, specifically asking about the use of focus groups with instructors and students, individual interviews with both groups, student course evaluations, survey instruments, and institutional data.

Among the respondents, the most common form of evaluation was the student course evaluation, but, as is evident in Table 5.1, campuses used a variety of other methods to evaluate their seminars. More often than not, if institutions used a survey instrument, it was one they created (86.7%) rather than an external instrument (26%).

Table 5.1
Types of Evaluation Methods Used (N = 322)

Type of evaluation	Two-year institution (*n* = 61)	Four-year institution (*n* = 261)	Total
Instructor focus groups	14	103	117
Student focus groups	13	92	105
Instructor interviews	10	49	59
Student interviews	6	37	43
Student course evaluations	52	233	285
Survey instruments	30	151	181
Institutional data	20	79	99

Note. Respondents could choose more than one option.

Since outcomes are tied to seminar types, Table 5.2 reports seminar outcomes in this way. Though respondents could select more than one response, it is still important to note that the assessments may or may not have been developed to assess other listed variables. Therefore, it is essential not to assume

Table 5.2
Outcomes Attributed to Participation in First-Year Seminars by Seminar Type ($n = 183$)

Outcomes	Types of Seminars				
	Extended orientation ($n = 159$)	Academic/ Uniform ($n = 68$)	Academic/ Variable ($n = 49$)	Basic study skills ($n = 13$)	Pre-profess-ional ($n = 10$)
Improved/ increased as a result of the seminar					
Peer connections	59.1%	53.0%	65.3%	46.2%	50.0%
Grade point average	33.3%	17.7%	16.3%	53.9%	10.0%
Academic abilities	27.6%	39.7%	55.1%	69.2%	40.0%
Involvement in campus activities	45.3%	42.7%	34.7%	30.8%	0.0%
Student/ faculty out-of-class interaction	40.9%	54.4%	49.0%	46.2%	20.0%
Persistence to sophomore year	62.9%	51.5%	51.0%	84.6%	60.0%
Persistence to graduation	18.2%	17.7%	14.3%	38.5%	10.0%
Satisfaction with faculty	25.2%	25.0%	51.0%	38.5%	40.0%
Satisfaction with institution	51.6%	50.0%	44.9%	53.9%	60.0%
Use of campus services	65.4%	39.7%	26.5%	53.9%	30.0%

Note. Respondents could choose more than one option; therefore, percentages do not equal 100%.

one type of seminar is more likely to achieve certain outcomes than another type of seminar, only that these were the outcomes that were measured and found to be improved or increased by seminar type.

For example, these findings suggest institutions with primarily basic study skills seminars were more likely to assess and see increased academic abilities than those offering primarily extended orientation seminars. It is not possible to determine from these data if basic study skill seminars are inherently more likely than another seminar type to achieve this outcome, only that this variable was assessed and found increased more often by the institutions that offered basic study skill seminars.

Nevertheless, some results were consistent across all seminar types. For example, persistence to the sophomore year was one of the most frequently reported outcomes in all five seminar types (i.e., 84.6% increase with basic study skills seminars, 62.9% increase with extended orientation seminars, 51% increase with academic seminars with variable content, 51.5% increase with academic seminars with uniform content, and 60% increase with pre-professional seminars). In addition, institutions reported that all seminar types increased satisfaction with the institution and improved peer connections.

However, increased persistence to graduation as a result of participation in the seminar is reported by relatively few of the responding institutions (i.e., academic seminar with variable content reported 14.3%, academic seminar with uniform content with 17.7%, extended orientation with 18.2%, and pre-professional with 10%), except those offering basic study skills seminars (38.5%). This finding may reflect either that institutions did not measure this variable or did not find that the seminar resulted in improved persistence to graduation.

A number of institutions offered a few additional outcomes. One institution found the seminars "helped to create a campus culture of support for first-year students." Another university mentioned that the seminar "increased student satisfaction with Orientation Week." This institution introduced the seminar during orientation; thus, tying those two experiences together benefited both orientation and the seminar at this school. Another college had the goal of increasing awareness of diversity and social justice issues and found through assessment that their first-year seminar was succeessful in achieving this goal. Finally, a few institutions mentioned improved student-staff relationships and improved advising. Seminars that have staff as instructors, instructors as advisors, and/or introduce students to campus staff and services may measure and see improvement in this area. These additional outcomes were offered anecdotally by participating institutions. It is impossible to determine the prevalence of these outcomes, because the survey did not specifically address these relationships or outcomes. Nevertheless, they reveal a wider range of potential outcomes assessed on individual campuses than those specifically listed on the survey.

Conclusion

This chapter explored the nature of institutional assessments on the first-year seminar. Although the most common method of assessment is the course evaluation, a number of campuses reported other methods they have used in recent years. The results show that, on many of the campuses, the seminar contributes to improved or increased peer connections, sophomore-year persistence, and student satisfaction with the institution. Depending on the seminar type, different outcomes may have been assessed. Thus, basic study skills seminars and academic seminars with variable content were more likely to report improved academic skills than other seminar types. It is unknown if institutions offering these seminars were also more likely to evaluate these academic skills than institutions offering different seminar types.

New Explorations Into Today's First-Year Seminar

6

The introduction and proliferation of online elements or courses, service-learning components, and learning communities have changed the first-year seminar in fundamental ways. Each of these elements has gained a solid foothold in first-year seminars since the last iteration of the survey. This chapter is dedicated to exploring these relatively new areas.

Online Elements in First-Year Seminars

For the first time, the 2003 seminar survey investigated how online elements were used in the course. We found that a number of the participating institutions offered entire sections or components of their first-year seminars in an online format. Both four-year (10.1%) and two-year institutions (21.6%) offered all or part of their seminars online.

Of the 81 institutions offering some aspect of their seminar online, 79 respondents provided insight into how their campuses used the Internet in the delivery of the course. Though some campuses offer only online versions, most campuses provided traditional classroom versions as well. Nevertheless, 31 institutions offered at least one section of a totally online first-year seminar. Ten institutions mentioned offering some type of hybrid course. These hybrids could be primarily online, offering only a few face-to-face sessions, or primarily classroom seminars, with some significant online elements.

Institutions offered a variety of online components in their first-year seminars. For example, 24 respondents (29.6%) identified using some course management system (e.g., Blackboard, WebCT, E-Companion). Others specified ways seminar instructors used these systems, including:

- Conducting discussion sessions (approximately 10%)
- E-mailing students (7.4%)
- Introducing students to the library (6.2%)
- Giving quizzes (3.7%)
- Introducing students to computers (3.7%)
- Posting reading assignments (3.7%)
- Posting the syllabus (3.7%)
- Posting assignments (2.5%)
- Providing study skills support (2.5%)
- Sharing documents for students to work together (2.5%)

Respondents also reported a range of other purposes or uses, such as chat rooms, orientation, notes, presentations, reflection papers, and course evaluations and other assessments.

Another interesting distinction was made by two institutions that mentioned using technology prior to the start of the school year to be in touch with new students. Once the students arrived on campus and classes officially started, these sections became traditional classroom-based first-year seminars. Because the above strategies come as a response to an open-ended question asking respondents who offered part or all of their seminar online to describe those elements, the percentages do not necessarily reflect the number of institutions that used technology in this way. The percentages only represent the number of respondents who thought to include these uses in response to the prompt. Clearly, more in-depth research is needed on the use of technology in first-year seminars.

Service-Learning Components in the First-Year Seminar

In the 2003 survey, we explored for the first time the use of a service-learning component in first-year seminars. Zlotkowski (2002) defines service-learning as "curriculum-based, academically structured and facilitated service activities" (p. x). However, he notes that others might "apply the term to any service activity with explicit learning objectives" or even as a "stylish synonym for 'community service'" (p. x). In the survey, we defined service-learning as "non-remunerative service as part of a course." Almost a quarter (23.7%) of all the survey respondents offered a service-learning component in their first-year seminar, the bulk of those were in four-year institutions (28.8% of four-year institutions versus 9.3% of two-year institutions). Almost all of the reporting institutions that included service-learning in their seminars offered some details about this component (95% or 139 out of 145 institutions). As these were open-ended responses rather than forced responses, it is impossible to determine the prevalence of any of these approaches. Nevertheless, we still can learn quite a bit about these offerings.

The service-learning component was frequently required. Even when it was required, it was not always an element in all the first-year seminar sections at an institution. One institution offered a handful of service-learning focused seminars, while instructors in other sections determined if they would include service-learning in their individual course curriculum. Typically, participating institutions described it as "volunteer" or "community" service; but in a few instances, the respondents mentioned tying the service to learning goals and/or requiring reflection papers. For instance, students studying animal science completed their service at an animal shelter, and education majors worked at local schools. The service-learning experiences lasted for as little as a lunch hour (in one case) to as much as 30 hours (two cases). The modal response was 10 hours (10 institutions) with daylong experiences mentioned by seven respondents.

A number of the respondents mentioned that the class participated as a group in the service-learning enterprise, but a few noted that the service was done by the individual student. The types of service listed by the responding institutions included the animal shelter work mentioned above, reading poetry to senior citizens, participating in a weeklong peace festival, or tutoring. In a few instances, the respondents stated that the work contributed to the students' final grades in the course. Clearly, there is no one way to include service-learning in the first-year seminar, and the reporting institutions have found many different ways to include it as an element in their seminars. Though their descriptions run counter to the strict definition offered by Zlotkowski, the participating institutions viewed service-learning, however they defined it, as a key component in their first-year seminars.

Learning Communities and the First-Year Seminar

We have investigated the integration of first-year seminars in learning communities in previous surveys; but in this instrument, we explored the topic in greater depth. The current instrument asks whether the first-year seminar is "linked to one or more other courses (i.e., 'learning community'—enrolling a cohort of students into two or more courses)." Gabelnick, MacGregor, Matthews, and Smith (1990) provide a more detailed definition: "Learning communities…purposefully restructure the curriculum to link together courses or course work so that students find greater coherence in what they are learning as well as increased intellectual interaction with faculty and fellow students" (p. 5).

Approximately one quarter (24.8%) of the survey participants noted that their first-year seminar is linked to one or more courses. Of those 152 institutions, most of the learning communities existed on the campuses of four-year institutions (79%). Almost all of the campuses with linked courses provided some details regarding their offerings.

Since the information regarding these curricular structures comes from unprompted responses, a great variety of topics were covered. Some of the survey participants discussed how many courses were linked: The first-year seminar was typically linked to two other courses. There were two distinct types of learning communities represented by responding institutions. First, courses were block scheduled. Students were in the same course with all or some of the same students, but the subjects were not integrated. Second, the course subjects were integrated so that thematic connections were made between linked courses. In some instances, participants stated that one of the linked courses was a developmental or skills course so that the skills learned in it were used in the other linked courses. Often, the respondents mentioned that some, but not all, of the first-year seminar sections were linked. Therefore, some of the first-year seminars were embedded in learning communities, but not all of them were structured in this way.

Additionally, a wide range of disciplines were linked to the first-year seminar, but the most common links were with English, composition, and/or reading (See Table 6.1). Interestingly, though some linked courses were developmental, providing academic support for less-prepared students, one survey participant mentioned that their institution's linked courses were part of a residential honors college. Therefore, learning communities, as described by survey participants, were used with both under-prepared and advanced students.

Table 6.1
Types of Courses Linked With the First-Year Seminar (N = 152)

Linked courses	Total number of institutions
English (i.e., writing, reading, composition)	30
Liberal arts (i.e., social sciences, history, western civilization, psychology, anthropology, philosophy, sociology)	24
Developmental courses (i.e., math, reading, writing, study skills)	16
Natural sciences (i.e., biology, health)	8
Computer sciences	3

Note. The table reports only the most frequently reported course linkages.

Only five of the institutions mentioned that the learning community was residential in nature. At five other institutions, the first-year learning community was associated with a Freshman Interest Group (FIG).[1] One community college offered a learning community for high school students taking community college courses. In this example, the students were enrolled in block college courses at the community college (including the first-year seminar), while completing their high school curriculum at their secondary school. Thus, learning communities on participating campuses included many different courses, in addition to first-year seminars, and were designed for a wide range of students.

Conclusion

This chapter looked at first-year seminars in terms of online components/courses, service-learning, and learning communities. These innovative approaches and components are becoming more prevalent in relation to first-year seminars. This survey instrument begins to understand how they are used, but much more research is needed. The next chapter provides significant detailed findings from the 2003 survey administration.

Notes

[1]These institutions did not provide their definition of a FIG; therefore, we use their term without understanding the specifics of their FIGs. Typically, FIGs are integrated linked courses.

References

Gabelnick, F., MacGregor, J., Matthews, R. S., & Smith, B. L. (Eds.). (1990). *Learning communities: Creating connections among students, faculty, and disciplines* (New Directions for Teaching and Learning No. 41). San Francisco: Jossey-Bass.

Zlotkowski, E. (Ed.). (2002). *Service-learning and the first-year experience: Preparing students for personal success and civic responsibility* (Monograph No. 34). Columbia, SC: University of South Carolina, National Resource Center for The First-Year Experience and Students in Transition.

Overview of Survey Responses

Bradley E. Cox

This chapter includes 88 tables presenting detailed results from the survey. Each section opens with a short narrative highlighting interesting results. The first table(s) in each category present data from across all institutions while subsequent tables are disaggregated by institutional affiliation, selectivity,[1] enrollment, and/or seminar type. For disaggregated data, only those tables that contain statistically significant differences are included in this chapter.

Characteristics of Responding, Non-Proprietary Institutions With Seminars

Of the 750 non-proprietary schools that responded to the survey, 621 had seminars. These 621 schools form our sample for the analysis presented in this chapter. While the sample is nearly equally split between public and private schools, the sample is predominantly small, four-year schools (see Table 7.1).

Table 7.1
Characteristics of Responding Institutions With Seminars (N = 621)

	Frequency	Percentage
Institutional type		
Two-year	163	26.3
Four-year	458	73.8
Institutional affiliation^		
Private	314	50.7
Public	306	49.4
Institutional enrollment		
5,000 or less	428	68.9
5,001 - 10,000	88	14.2
10,001 - 15,000	43	6.9
15,001 - 20,000	32	5.2
More than 20,000	30	4.8

^One school did not indicate its affiliation.

Course Longevity

Table 7.2 presents the number of years that institutions have offered their first-year seminars. Nearly all of the responding institutions indicated that their seminars were at least three years old.

Table 7.2
Seminar Longevity Across All Institutions (N = 608)

	Frequency	Percentage
Two years or less	53	8.7
Three to 10 years	305	50.2
More than 10 years	250	41.1

Types of Seminars Offered

Since the 1991 survey administration, the National Resource Center has defined five types of first-year seminars (see chapter 1 for definitions). The 2003 survey asked respondents to indicate which types of seminars were offered on their campuses. The majority of these institutions (65.2%) offered an extended orientation seminar. Academic seminars, both those with uniform content and those with variable content across sections, were also frequently offered (27.4% and 24.3%, respectively). A number of schools indicated that they offered more than one type of first-year seminar.

When examined by institutional affiliation (public vs. private), institutional type (two-year vs. four-year), and admission selectivity, a number of distinctions became apparent. Extended orientation and basic study skills seminars were significantly more frequent in public, two-year institutions and those that were not highly selective. Academic seminars—both those with uniform content and those with variable content—were more common at private and four-year schools (see Tables 7.3 - 7.6).

Table 7.3
Respondents Offering Each Type of Seminar Across All Institutions (N = 620)

	Frequency	Percentage
Extended orientation (EO)	405	65.2
Academic (uniform content) (AUC)	170	27.4
Academic (variable content) (AVC)	151	24.3
Basic study skills (BSS)	124	20.0
Pre-professional (PRE)	88	14.2
Other	51	8.2

Note. Percentages do not equal 100%. Respondents could make more than one selection.

Table 7.4
Percentage of Respondents Offering Each Type of Seminar by Institutional Affiliation (N = 620)

	Private (n = 314)	Public (n = 306)
Extended orientation**	53.5	77.1
Academic (uniform content)**	34.4	19.9
Academic (variable content)*	28.3	20.3
Basic study skills**	10.5	29.7
Pre-professional**	8.9	19.6
Other*	10.5	5.9

Note. Percentages do not equal 100%. Respondents could make more than one selection.
*$p < .05$
**$p < .01$

Table 7.5
Percentage of Respondents Offering Each Type of Seminar by Institutional Type
(*N* = 621)

	Two-year (*n* = 163)	Four-year (*n* = 458)
Extended orientation**	79.8	60.0
Academic (uniform content)**	18.4	30.6
Academic (variable content)**	7.4	30.4
Basic study skills**	37.4	13.8
Pre-professional	10.4	15.5
Other*	5.5	9.2

Note. Percentages do not equal 100%. Respondents could make more than one selection.
*$p < .05$
**$p < .01$

Table 7.6
Percentage of Respondents Offering Each Type of Seminar by Institutional Selectivity
(*N* = 621)

	High (*n* = 56)	Other (*n* = 565)
Extended orientation**	21.4	69.6
Academic (uniform content)	32.1	26.9
Academic (variable content)**	67.9	20.0
Basic study skills**	0.0	22.0
Pre-professional	7.1	14.9
Other	7.1	8.3

Note. Percentages do not equal 100%. Respondents could make more than one selection.
**$p < .01$

Primary Seminar Types

Though a number of schools offered more than one seminar type, respondents were asked to complete the survey based on the seminar type with the highest total enrollment. While the extended orientation seminar was most frequently cited as having the highest enrollment for all types of schools, significant differences were found between public and private schools and between two-year and four-year schools (see Tables 7.7 - 7.9).

Table 7.7
Respondents' Primary Seminar Type Across All Institutions (N = 603)

	Frequency	Percentage
Extended orientation	303	50.3
Academic (uniform content)	120	19.9
Academic (variable content)	102	16.9
Basic study skills	34	5.6
Pre-professional	17	2.8
Other	27	4.5

Table 7.8
Percentage of Respondents Reporting Primary Seminar Type by Institutional Affiliation (N = 602)

	Private (n = 305)	Public (n = 297)
Extended orientation	38.7	62.3
Academic (uniform content)	28.5	10.8
Academic (variable content)	23.0	10.8
Basic study skills	2.6	8.8
Pre-professional	2.0	3.7
Other	5.3	3.7

$p < .01$

Table 7.9
Percentage of Respondents Reporting Primary Seminar Type by Institutional Type
(*N* = 603)

	Two-year (*n* = 158)	Four-year (*n* = 445)
Extended orientation	69.6	43.4
Academic (uniform content)	10.1	23.4
Academic (variable content)	1.3	22.5
Basic study skills	15.2	2.3
Pre-professional	1.9	3.2
Other	1.9	5.4

p < .01

Class Size

The 2003 survey queried respondents about their class size. Most schools indicated that their seminars had approximate class sizes of either between 16 and 20 students (36.1%) or 21 and 25 students (33.7%). Both private and highly selective schools were more likely to have class sizes of 20 or fewer students (see Tables 7.10 - 7.12).

Table 7.10
Percentage of Respondents Reporting Approximate Class Size Across All Institutions
(*N* = 618)

	Frequency	Percentage
Under 10	7	1.1
10 - 15	106	17.2
16 - 20	223	36.1
21 - 25	208	33.7
Other	74	12.0

Table 7.11
Percentage of Respondents Reporting Approximate Class Size by Institutional Affiliation (N = 617)

	Private (*n* = 313)	Public (*n* = 304)
Under 10	1.6	0.7
10 - 15	27.2	6.9
16 - 20	43.1	28.9
21 - 25	20.8	46.7
Other	7.3	16.8

p < .01

Table 7.12
Percentage of Respondents Reporting Approximate Class Size by Institutional Selectivity (N = 618)

	High (*n* = 56)	Other (*n* = 562)
Under 10	0.0	1.2
10 - 15	33.9	15.5
16 - 20	55.4	34.2
21 - 25	10.7	35.9
Other	0.0	13.2

p < .01

Seminar as Required Course

Nearly half (46.8%) of responding institutions required all of their first-year students to take the first-year seminar. Conversely, at nearly 20% of the schools, the course was not required for any student. Private schools were more likely than public schools to require the course for all its first-year students (68.1% and 24.9%, respectively) (see Tables 7.13 - 7.16).

Table 7.13
Percentage of First-Year Students Required to Take Seminar Across All Institutions
(N = 615)

	Frequency	Percentage
100%	288	46.8
90 - 99%	53	8.6
80 - 89%	17	2.8
70 - 79%	21	3.4
60 - 69%	16	2.6
50 - 59%	5	0.8
Less than 50%	93	15.1
0%	122	19.8

Table 7.14
Percentage of First-Year Students Required to Take Seminar by Institutional
Affiliation (N = 614)

	Private (n = 313)	Public (n = 301)
100%	68.1	24.9
90 - 99%	10.5	6.6
80 - 89%	1.6	4.0
70 - 79%	2.2	4.3
60 - 69%	1.9	3.3
50 - 59%	0.0	1.7
Less than 50%	6.7	23.9
0%	8.9	31.2

$p < .01$

Table 7.15
Type of Students Required to Take Seminar Across All Institutions (N = 333)

	Frequency	Percentage
Provisionally admitted students	69	20.7
Learning community participants	42	12.6
Undeclared students	37	11.1
Student athletes	35	10.5
Honors students	27	8.1
Students in specific majors	25	7.5
Other	107	32.1
None	123	37.0

Note. Percentages do not equal 100%. Respondents could make more than one selection.

Table 7.16
Type of Students Required to Take Seminar by Institutional Selectivity (N = 333)

	High (*n* = 24)	Other (*n* = 309)
Provisionally admitted students*	4.2	22.0
Learning community participants	12.5	12.6
Undeclared students	4.2	11.7
Student athletes	8.3	10.7
Honors students	12.5	7.8
Students in specific majors	0.0	8.1
Other	29.2	32.4
None	54.2	35.6

Note. Percentages do not equal 100%. Respondents could make more than one selection.
*$p < .05$

Special Sections of Seminar

A number of schools indicated that special sections of the seminar were offered to specific student populations. Over 20% of schools offered special sections for academically underprepared students, while 18.2% offered sections specifically designed for honor students. Public schools and larger schools (those with more than 5,000 students) were more likely to offer special sections than private and small schools (see Tables 7.17 - 7.20).

Table 7.17
Percentage of Special Sections Offered Across All Institutions (N = 621)

	Frequency	Percentage
Academically underprepared students	128	20.6
Honors students	113	18.2
Learning community participants	95	15.3
Students within a specific major	92	14.8
Undeclared students	47	7.6
Pre-professional students	42	6.8
Transfer students	34	5.5
International students	31	5.0
Students residing within a particular residence hall	31	5.0
Other	56	9.0
No special sections are offered	278	44.8

Note. Percentages do not equal 100%. Respondents could make more than one selection.

Table 7.18

Percentage of Special Sections Offered by Institutional Affiliation (N = 620)

	Private (*n* = 314)	Public (*n* = 306)
Academically underprepared students**	14.0	27.5
Honors students	16.6	19.9
Learning community participants**	7.3	23.5
Students within a specific major**	11.2	18.6
Undeclared students*	5.1	10.1
Pre-professional students	4.8	8.5
Transfer students	6.4	4.6
International students	5.7	4.3
Students residing within a particular residence hall**	2.6	7.5
Other	7.0	11.1
No special sections are offered**	55.4	34.0

Note. Percentages do not equal 100%. Respondents could make more than one selection.
*$p < .05$
**$p < .01$

Table 7.19
Percentage of Special Sections Offered by Institutional Enrollment (N = 621)

	5,000 or less	5,001- 10,000	10,001- 15,000	15,001- 20,000	More than 20,000
	(*n* = 428)	(*n* = 88)	(*n* = 43)	(*n* = 32)	(*n* = 30)
Academically underprepared students**	16.4	35.2	18.6	28.1	33.3
Honors students*	15.2	23.9	18.6	28.1	33.3
Learning community participants**	9.1	23.9	16.3	43.8	46.7
Students within a specific major*	12.2	17.1	20.9	31.3	20.0
Undeclared students	5.6	13.6	9.3	9.4	13.3
Pre-professional students	4.9	13.6	2.3	15.6	10.0
Transfer students	4.4	8.0	7.0	9.4	6.7
International students	4.4	5.7	7.0	6.3	6.7
Students residing within a particular residence hall	2.6	5.7	4.7	9.4	33.3
Other	5.8	18.2	16.3	18.8	6.7
No special sections are offered**	52.3	30.7	37.2	12.5	23.3

Note. Percentages do not equal 100%. Respondents could make more than one selection.
*$p < .05$
**$p < .01$

Table 7.20
Percentage of Special Sections Offered by Institutional Selectivity (N = 621)

	High (n = 56)	Other (n = 565)
Academically underprepared students**	1.8	5.8
Honors students	16.1	18.4
Learning community participants	12.5	15.6
Students within a specific major	7.1	15.6
Undeclared students*	0.0	8.3
Pre-professional students	3.6	7.1
Transfer students	1.8	5.8
International students	7.1	4.8
Students residing within a particular residence hall	5.4	5.0
Other	10.7	8.9
No special sections are offered	51.8	44.1

Note. Percentages do not equal 100%. Respondents could make more than one selection.
*$p < .05$
**$p < .01$

Teaching Responsibility

A strong majority of responding institutions used faculty to teach their seminar sections (89.9%). Student affairs professionals and other campus professionals (e.g., librarians and academic administrators) were also used at a number of campuses (45.2% and 30.9%, respectively). Private schools were less likely than public schools to use student affairs professionals (38.2% vs. 52.6%) and/or graduate students (1.6% vs. 7.2%). Nearly all of the highly selective schools used faculty to teach their seminars (98.2%) (see Tables 7.21 - 7.23).

Table 7.21
Teaching Responsibility Across All Institutions (N = 621)

	Frequency	Percentage
Faculty	558	89.9
Student affairs professionals	281	45.2
Other campus professionals	192	30.9
Graduate students	27	4.3
Undergraduate students	39	6.3

Note. Percentages do not equal 100%. Respondents could make more than one selection.

Table 7.22
Teaching Responsibility by Institutional Affiliation (N=620)

	Private (n = 314)	Public (n = 306)
Faculty	90.8%	88.9%
Student affairs professionals**	38.2%	52.6%
Other campus professionals	28.3%	33.7%
Graduate students**	1.6%	7.2%
Undergraduate students**	9.2%	3.3%

Note. Percentages do not equal 100%. Respondents could make more than one selection.
**$p < .01$

Table 7.23
Teaching Responsibility by Institutional Selectivity (N = 621)

	Highly Selective (n = 56)	Other (n = 565)
Faculty*	98.2%	89.0%
Student affairs professionals**	14.3%	48.3%
Other campus professionals*	17.9%	32.2%
Graduate students	1.8%	4.6%
Undergraduate students	1.8%	6.7%

Note. Percentages do not equal 100%. Respondents could make more than one selection.
*$p < .05$
**$p < .01$

Team Teaching

Respondents were asked two questions regarding the use of team teaching in their seminars. First, they were asked if any seminar sections were team taught. They were then asked what percent of the sections were team taught. While 39.3% of the schools reported offering some sections employing team teaching, most schools (56.4%) used team teaching in less than 25% of their sections. Private schools were more likely than public schools to team teach all of their sections (35.0% and 18.6%, respectively) (see Tables 7.24 - 7.27).

Table 7.24
Percentage of Institutions Reporting Team-Taught Sections Across All Institutions (N = 615)

	Frequency	Percentage
Yes	242	39.3
No	373	60.7

Table 7.25
Percentage of Students Enrolled in Team-Taught Sections Across All Institutions
(N = 241)

	Frequency	Percentage
100%	64	26.6
75 - 99%	9	3.7
50 - 74%	12	5.0
25 - 49%	20	8.3
Less than 25%	136	56.4

Table 7.26
Percentage of Students Team Taught by Institutional Affiliation (N = 241)

	Private (n = 117)	Public (n = 124)
100%	35.0	18.6
75 - 99%	2.6	4.8
50 - 74%	6.0	4.0
25 - 49%	8.6	8.1
Less than 25%	47.9	64.5

$p < .05$

Table 7.27
Team Teaching by Seminar Type (N = 599)

	EO (n = 302)	AUC (n = 120)	AVC (n = 100)	BSS (n = 33)	PRE (n = 17)	Other (n = 27)
Frequency	118	39	45	8	9	17
Percentage	39.1	32.5	45.0	24.2	52.9	63.0

$p < .05$

Connection to Academic Advising

Fewer than one third (30.4%) of the schools intentionally placed any of their students in sections taught by their academic advisors. The intentional use of academic advisors as instructors was more frequent in private schools (36.1% vs. 24.7%) and in highly selective schools (44.6% vs. 29.0%). Private schools were also more likely to enroll greater than three-fourths of their students in sections taught by the students' academic advisor (62.6% vs. 25.0%) (see Tables 7.28 - 7.32).

Table 7.28
Institutions with Sections Taught by Academic Advisor Across All Institutions
$(N = 618)$

	Frequency	Percentage
Yes	188	30.4
No	430	69.6

Table 7.29
Institutions with Sections Taught by Academic Advisor by Institutional Affiliation
$(N = 617)$

	Private ($n = 313$)	Public ($n = 304$)
Frequency	113	75
Percentage	36.1	24.7

$p < .01$

Table 7.30
Institutions with Sections Taught by Academic Advisor by Institutional Selectivity
$(N = 618)$

	High ($n = 56$)	Other ($n = 562$)
Frequency	25	163
Percentage	44.6	29.0

$p < .05$

Table 7.31
Percentage of Students Enrolled in Sections Taught by Academic Advisors Across All Institutions (N = 179)

	Frequency	Percentage
76 - 100%	85	47.5
51 - 75%	14	7.8
25 - 50%	38	21.2
Less than 25%	42	23.5

Table 7.32
Percentage of Students Enrolled in Sections Taught by Academic Advisor by Institutional Affiliation (N = 179)

	Private (*n* = 107)	Public (*n* = 72)
76 - 100%	62.6	25.0
51 - 75%	4.7	12.5
25 - 50%	16.8	27.8
Less than 25%	15.9	34.7

$p < .01$

Teaching Workload and Compensation

Survey respondents were asked to indicate how teaching the first-year seminar was configured as a part of faculty and staff workloads. Respondents could select more than one configuration. Across all institutions, teaching the first-year seminar was most often considered a part of the regular teaching load for faculty (68.8%), while it was most often an extra responsibility for staff teaching the course (58.9%). Highly selective institutions were also likely to consider teaching the first-year seminar part of the regular teaching load for faculty (81.8%) but as an extra responsibility for administrative staff (86.7%).

The majority (83.1%) of institutions that responded to our inquiry about compensation offered stipends for instructors, but only 8.7% offered release time. Private institutions were more likely than public schools to compensate instructors with a stipend (79.9% and 69.7%, respectively), while public schools were more likely than private schools to offer release time (12.9% and 4.3%, respectively). Chapter 4 offers a more detailed discussion on the amount of remuneration offered (see Tables 7.33 - 7.40).

Table 7.33
Faculty Workload Configuration Across All Institutions (N = 558)

	Frequency	Percentage
Part of regular teaching load	384	68.8
Overload course	221	39.6
Other	54	9.7

Note. Percentages do not equal 100%. Respondents could make more than one selection.

Table 7.34
Faculty Workload Configuration by Institutional Selectivity (N = 558)

	High (n = 55)	Other (n = 503)
Part of regular teaching load*	81.8%	67.4%
Overload course*	23.6%	41.4%
Other	7.3%	9.9%

Note. Percentages do not equal 100%. Respondents could make more than one selection.
*$p < .05$

Table 7.35
Faculty Workload Configuration by Seminar Type (N = 541)

	EO (n = 255)	AUC (n = 116)	AVC (n = 101)	BSS (n = 29)	PRE (n = 17)	Other (n = 23)
Part of regular teaching load**	56.1%	81.9%	82.2%	86.2%	58.8%	73.9%
Overload course**	47.1%	37.1%	24.8%	31.0%	35.3%	30.4%
Other*	13.3%	6.0%	5.9%	0.0%	5.9%	21.7%

Note. Percentages do not equal 100%. Respondents could make more than one selection.
*$p < .05$
**$p < .01$

Table 7.36
Administrative Staff Workload Configuration Across All Institutions (N = 355)

	Frequency	Percentage
Assigned responsibility	148	41.7
Extra responsibility	209	58.9
Other	40	11.3

Note. Percentages do not equal 100%. Respondents could make more than one selection.

Table 7.37
Administrative Staff Workload Configuration by Enrollment (N = 355)

	5,000 or less	5,001 - 10,000	10,001 - 15,000	15,001 - 20,000	More than 20,000
	(*n* = 231)	(*n* = 56)	(*n* = 26)	(*n* = 24)	(*n* = 18)
Assigned responsibility	41.1%	41.1%	46.2%	33.3%	55.6%
Extra responsibility**	64.9%	41.1%	61.5%	58.3%	33.3%
Other	6.5%	23.2%	11.5%	20.8%	22.2%

Note. Percentages do not equal 100%. Respondents could make more than one selection.
**$p < .01$

Table 7.38
Administrative Staff Workload Configuration by Institutional Selectivity (N = 355)

	High	Other
	(*n* = 15)	(*n* = 340)
Assigned responsibilty	26.7%	42.4%
Extra responsibility*	86.7%	57.7%
Other	0.0%	11.8%

Note. Percentages do not equal 100%. Respondents could make more than one selection.
*$p < .05$

Table 7.39
Instructor Compensation Across All Institutions (N = 343)

	Frequency	Percentage
Stipend	285	83.1
Release time	30	8.7
Graduate student support	3	0.9
Other	50	14.6

Note. Percentages do not equal 100%. Respondents could make more than one selection.

Table 7.40
Instructor Compensation by Institutional Affiliation (N = 342)

	Private (*n* = 164)	Public (*n* = 178)
Stipend*	79.9%	69.7%
Release time**	4.3%	12.9%
Graduate student support	0.0%	1.7%

Note. Percentages do not equal 100%. Respondents could make more than one selection.
*$p < .05$
**$p < .01$

Instructor Training

Nearly three fourths (72.4%) of the institutions offered instructor training. Of those who offered training, 68.8% required it. Most training sessions were short, with 36.1% lasting half a day or less, 22.8% lasting one day, and 17.8% lasting two days. Only half (50.0%) of the highly selective responding institutions required instructors to attend training; 70.6% of the other institutions required the training (see Tables 7.41 - 7.45).

Table 7.41
Instructor Training Offered Across All Institutions (N = 612)

	Frequency	Percentage
Yes	443	72.4
No	169	27.6

Table 7.42
Instructor Training Offered by Seminar Type (N = 595)

	EO	AUC	AVC	BSS	PRE	Other
	(*n* = 299)	(*n* = 119)	(*n* = 101)	(*n* = 33)	(*n* = 16)	(*n* = 27)
Frequency	214	97	75	15	7	22
Percentage	71.6	81.5	74.3	45.5	43.8	81.5

$p < .01$

Table 7.43
Instructor Training Required Across All Institutions (N = 439)

	Frequency	Percentage
Yes	302	68.8
No	137	31.2

Table 7.44
Instructor Training Required by Institutional Selectivity (N = 439)

	High	Other
	(*n* = 38)	(*n* = 401)
Frequency	19	283
Percentage	50.0	70.6

$p < .05$

Table 7.45
Length of Instructor Training Across All Institutions (N = 443)

	Frequency	Percentage
Half day or less	160	36.1
One day	101	22.8
Two days	79	17.8
Three days	23	5.2
Four days	9	2.0
One week	14	3.2
Other	85	19.2

Academic Credit and Grading

At most schools (89.9%), the first-year seminar carried academic credit. Most frequently offered for one credit-hour (49.5%) or three credit-hours (31.2%), seminars were generally letter graded (78.9%). Credit was most frequently applicable as either a general education requirement (57.2%) or as an elective (42.0%).

The course was more likely to count toward general education requirements at private and highly selective institutions (75.1% and 72.7%, respectively) than it was at their public and less-selective counterparts (38.0% and 55.5%, respectively). The majority of extended orientation (65.7%) and pre-professional/discipline-based seminars (62.5%) carried one credit-hour (see Tables 7.46 - 7.54).

Table 7.46
Percentage of Seminars That Carry Credit Toward Graduation Across All Institutions (N = 618)

	Frequency	Percentage
Yes	552	89.3
No	66	10.7

Table 7.47
Percentage of Seminars That Carry Credit Toward Graduation by Institutional Selectivity (N = 618)

	High	Other
	(*n* = 56)	(*n* = 562)
Frequency	55	497
Percentage	98.2	88.4

$p < .05$

Table 7.48
Application of Credit Across All Institutions (N = 552)

	Frequency	Percentage
General education	316	57.2
As an elective	232	42.0
Major	33	6.0
Other	44	8.0

Note. Percentages do not equal 100%. Respondents could make more than one selection.

Table 7.49
Application of Credit by Institutional Affiliation (N = 551)

	Private	Public
	(*n* = 285)	(*n* = 266)
General education**	75.1%	38.0%
As an elective**	23.9%	61.7%
Major	5.3%	6.8%
Other	6.3%	9.8%

Note. Percentages do not equal 100%. Respondents could make more than one selection.
**$p < .01$

Table 7.50
Application of Credit by Institutional Selectivity ($N = 552$)

	High	Other
	($n = 55$)	($n = 497$)
General education*	72.7%	55.5%
As an elective	30.9%	43.3%
Major	9.1%	5.6%
Other	10.9%	7.7%

Note. Percentages do not equal 100%. Respondents could make more than one selection.
*$p < .05$

Table 7.51
Credit Hours Offered Across All Institutions ($N = 552$)

	Frequency	Percentage
One	273	49.5
Two	73	13.2
Three	172	31.2
Four	51	9.2
Five	7	1.3
More than five	14	2.5

Note. Percentages do not equal 100%. Respondents could make more than one selection.

Table 7.52
Credit Hours Offered by Institutional Selectivity (N = 552)

	High (n = 55)	Other (n = 497)
One**	30.9%	51.5%
Two	5.5%	14.1%
Three	30.9%	31.2%
Four**	30.9%	6.8%
Five	3.6%	1.0%
More than five*	7.3%	2.0%

Note. Percentages do not equal 100%. Respondents could make more than one selection.
*$p < .05$
**$p < .01$

Table 7.53
Credit Hours Offered by Seminar Type (N = 537)

	EO (n = 251)	AUC (n = 114)	AVC (n = 102)	BSS (n = 27)	PRE (n = 16)	Other (n = 27)
One**	65.7%	37.7%	21.6%	40.7%	62.5%	44.4%
Two	15.9%	10.5%	5.9%	18.5%	18.8%	18.5%
Three**	22.7%	37.7%	44.1%	48.2%	18.8%	22.2%
Four	0.0%	14.0%	30.4%	0.0%	6.3%	11.1%
Five	0.4%	0.9%	3.9%	0.0%	0.0%	3.7%
More than five	0.8%	5.3%	2.0%	3.7%	0.0%	11.1%

**$p < .01$

Table 7.54
Method of Grading Across All Institutions (N = 620)

	Frequency	Percentage
Letter grade	489	78.9
Pass/fail	115	18.5
No grade	16	2.6

Seminar Length and Contact Hours

Most seminars (76.5%) lasted one semester. Three contact hours per week was the most common among institutions responding (36.1%), but 34.3% of respondents had seminars with one contact hour per week, while an additional 20.9% had two. Highly selective schools tended to offer seminars with more contact hours; 75% of the highly selective schools offered three or more contact hours per week (see Tables 7.55 - 7.58).

Table 7.55
Seminar Length Across All Institutions (N = 621)

	Frequency	Percentage
One semester	475	76.5
One quarter	35	5.6
One year	52	8.4

Table 7.56
Contact Hours Per Week Across All Institutions (N = 621)

	Frequency	Percentage
One	213	34.3
Two	130	20.9
Three	224	36.1
Four	39	6.3
Five	8	1.3
More than five	23	3.7

Table 7.57
Contact Hours by Institutional Selectivity (N = 621)

	High (n = 56)	Other (n = 565)
One**	17.9%	35.9%
Two**	7.1%	22.3%
Three*	50.0%	34.7%
Four**	19.6%	5.0%
Five	3.6%	1.1%
More than five	7.1%	3.4%

*$p < .05$
**$p < .01$

Table 7.58
Contact Hours Per Week by Seminar Type (N = 603)

	EO	AUC	AVC	BSS	PRE	Other
	(n = 303)	(n = 120)	(n = 102)	(n = 34)	(n = 17)	(n = 27)
One**	46.5%	24.2%	10.8%	23.5%	41.2%	37.0%
Two*	25.4%	18.3%	9.8%	20.6%	23.5%	14.8%
Three*	25.4%	45.0%	54.9%	50.0%	35.3%	33.3%
Four	0.7%	9.2%	20.6%	0.0%	5.9%	14.8%
Five	0.3%	3.3%	2.0%	0.0%	0.0%	3.7%
More than five	3.3%	0.8%	6.9%	8.8%	0.0%	7.4%

$*p < .05$
$**p < .01$

Service-Learning and Learning Communities

Approximately one quarter (23.7%) of the responding institutions included a service-learning component in their seminars; 24.8% indicated that their seminars were linked to other courses to form learning communities. While private schools were twice as likely to include service-learning as their public counterparts (32.0% and 15.2%, respectively), they were only one half as likely to include the seminar as part of a learning community (15.2% and 34.8%, respectively) (see Tables 7.59 - 7.65). Service-learning and learning communities are discussed in greater detail in chapter 6.

Table 7.59
Seminar Includes Service-Learning Component Across All Institutions (N = 612)

	Frequency	Percentage
Yes	145	23.7
No	467	76.3

Table 7.60
Seminar Includes Service-Learning Component by Institutional Affiliation (N = 611)

	Private (*n* = 309)	Public (*n* = 302)
Frequency	99	46
Percentage	32.0	15.2

$p < .01$

Table 7.61
Seminar Includes Service-Learning Component by Institutional Enrollment
(N = 612)

	5,000 or less (*n* = 421)	5,001 - 10,000 (*n* = 88)	10,001 - 15,000 (*n* = 42)	15,001 - 20,000 (*n* = 31)	More than 20,000 (*n* = 30)
Frequency	118	10	5	8	4
Percentage	28.0	11.4	11.9	25.8	13.3

$p < .05$

Table 7.62
Seminar Includes Service-Learning Component by Seminar Type (N = 595)

	EO (*n* = 302)	AUC (*n* = 119)	AVC (*n* = 97)	BSS (*n* = 34)	PRE (*n* = 16)	Other (*n* = 27)
Frequency	69	36	23	2	1	9
Percentage	22.9	30.3	23.7	5.9	6.3	33.3

*$p < .05$

Table 7.63
Seminar is Part of Learning Community Across All Institutions (N = 613)

	Frequency	Percentage
Yes	152	24.8
No	461	75.2

Table 7.64
Seminar is Part of Learning Community by Institutional Affiliation (N = 612)

	Private (n = 310)	Public (n = 302)
Frequency	47	105
Percentage	15.2	34.8

$p < .01$

Table 7.65
Seminar is Part of Learning Community by Institutional Enrollment (N = 613)

	5,000 or less (n = 422)	5,001 - 10,000 (n = 88)	10,001 - 15,000 (n = 42)	15,001 - 20,000 (n = 31)	More than 20,000 (n = 30)
Frequency	77	31	14	14	16
Percentage	18.3	35.2	33.3	45.2	53.3

$p < .01$

Administration: Departmental and Individual Leadership

The unit most frequently cited as directly administering the seminars was academic affairs (46.2%). Seminars were administered by first-year program offices at only 10.5% of the responding institutions. While more than three fourths (77.3%) of respondents indicated that the seminar had a director/coordinator, this position was most frequently less than full-time (66.0%). Most of the directors/coordinators with other positions were members of the faculty (51.1%). The administrative home of the seminar and the existence and status of a coordinator/director varied by seminar type, institutional affiliation, and enrollment (see Tables 7.66 - 7.77).

Table 7.66
Administrative Home of First-Year Seminar Across All Institutions (N = 621)

	Frequency	Percentage
Academic affairs	287	46.2
Student affairs	129	20.8
Academic department	99	15.9
First-year program office	65	10.5
Other	94	15.1

Note. Percentages do not equal 100%. Respondents could make more than one selection.

Table 7.67
Administrative Home of First-Year Seminar by Institutional Affiliation (N = 620)

	Private (n = 314)	Public (n = 306)
Academic affairs**	52.9%	39.5%
Student affairs	18.2%	23.5%
Academic department*	12.7%	19.0%
First-year program office	9.2%	11.8%
Other	16.9%	13.4%

Note. Percentages do not equal 100%. Respondents could make more than one selection.
*$p < .05$
**$p < .01$

Table 7.68
Administrative Home of First-Year Seminar by Institutional Enrollment (N = 621)

	5,000 or less	5,001 - 10,000	10,001 - 15,000	15,001 - 20,000	More than 20,000
	(*n* = 428)	(*n* = 88)	(*n* = 43)	(*n* = 32)	(*n* = 30)
Academic affairs*	50.5%	37.5%	34.9%	34.4%	40.0%
Student affairs	20.8%	21.6%	20.9%	28.1%	10.0%
Academic department	14.7%	17.1%	23.3%	18.8%	16.7%
First-year program office	7.7%	17.1%	11.6%	21.9%	16.7%
Other	14.5%	15.9%	14.0%	9.4%	30.0%

Note. Percentages do not equal 100%. Respondents could make more than one selection.
*$p < .05$

Table 7.69
Administrative Home of First-Year Seminar by Seminar Type (N = 603)

	EO	AUC	AVC	BSS	PRE	Other
	(*n* = 303)	(*n* = 120)	(*n* = 102)	(*n* = 34)	(*n* = 17)	(*n* = 27)
Academic affairs**	36.3%	55.8%	60.8%	58.8%	41.2%	51.9%
Student affairs**	33.3%	10.8%	2.0%	8.8%	5.9%	14.8%
Academic department*	14.9%	20.0%	7.8%	23.5%	35.3%	14.8%
First-year program office	10.2%	8.3%	14.7%	8.8%	17.7%	11.1%
Other	13.5%	15.0%	19.6%	8.8%	11.8%	25.9%

Note. Percentages do not equal 100%. Respondents could make more than one selection.
*$p < .05$
**$p < .01$

Table 7.70
Seminar Has Director/Coordinator Across All Institutions (N = 617)

	Frequency	Percentage
Yes	477	77.3
No	140	22.7

Table 7.71
Seminar Has Director/Coordinator by Institutional Affiliation (N = 616)

	Private (n = 312)	Public (n = 304)
Frequency	259	218
Percentage	83.0	71.7

$p < .01$

Table 7.72
Seminar Has Director/Coordinator by Institutional Enrollment (N = 617)

	5,000 or less (n = 425)	5,001 - 10,000 (n = 88)	10,001 - 15,000 (n = 43)	15,001 - 20,000 (n = 32)	More than 20,000 (n = 29)
Frequency	331	62	30	31	23
Percentage	77.9	70.5	69.8	96.9	79.3

$p < .05$

Table 7.73
Seminar Has Director/Coordinator by Seminar Type (N = 600)

	EO (n = 301)	AUC (n = 119)	AVC (n = 102)	BSS (n = 34)	PRE (n = 17)	Other (n = 27)
Frequency	227	103	83	24	10	18
Percentage	75.4	86.6	81.4	70.6	58.8	66.7

$p < .05$

Table 7.74
Status of Director/Coordinator Across All Institutions (N = 476)

	Frequency	Percentage
Full time	162	34.0
Less than full time	314	66.0

Table 7.75
Status of Director/Coordinator by Institutional Affiliation (N = 476)

	Private (n = 259)	Public (n = 217)
Full time	27.4%	41.9%
Less than full time	72.6%	58.1%

$p < .01$

Table 7.76
Status of Director/Coordinator by Seminar Type (N = 464)

	EO (n = 227)	AUC (n = 103)	AVC (n = 83)	BSS (n = 24)	PRE (n = 9)	Other (n = 18)
Full time	38.8%	24.3%	24.1%	58.3%	55.6%	33.3%
Less than full time	61.2%	75.7%	75.9%	41.7%	44.4%	66.7%

$p < .01$

Table 7.77
Other Role of Director/Coordinator Across All Institutions (N = 315)

	Frequency	Percentage
Faculty member	161	51.1
Academic affairs administrator	86	27.3
Student affairs administrator	50	15.9
Other	47	14.9

Course Objectives

Survey respondents were asked to select the three most important objectives of their seminars. The two most frequently selected objectives were to develop academic skills (63.4%) and to orient students to campus resources and services (59.6%). Retention to the sophomore year was selected by 26.7% of the survey's respondents.

Course objective responses varied significantly by seminar type, institutional affiliation, and selectivity. The objectives of orienting to campus services and to develop a support network/friendships were most frequently reported by institutions with extended orientation seminars (80.2% and 45.5%, respectively). Increasing student/faculty interaction was most frequently selected by schools whose seminars were primarily academic seminars with variable content (57.8%) and by schools that were highly selective (60.7%) (see Tables 7.78 - 7.81).

Table 7.78
Most Important Course Objectives Across All Institutions (N = 621)

	Frequency	Percentage
Develop academic skills	394	63.4
Orient to campus resources & services	370	59.6
Encourage self-exploration/personal development	247	39.8
Develop support network/friendships	230	37.0
Create common first-year experience	224	36.1
Increase student/faculty interaction	194	31.2
Improve sophomore return rates	166	26.7
Introduce a discipline	45	7.2
Other	59	9.5

Note. Percentages do not equal 100%. Respondents were asked to select three most important objectives.

Table 7.79

Most Important Course Objectives by Institutional Affiliation (N = 620)

	Private (n = 314)	Public (n = 306)
Develop academic skills	59.9%	67.0%
Orient to campus resources & services*	51.9%	67.3%
Encourage self-exploration/personal development	37.6%	41.8%
Develop support network/friendships	35.7%	38.6%
Create common first-year experience**	44.6%	27.5%
Increase student/faculty interaction	33.8%	28.8%
Improve sophomore return rates*	22.9%	30.7%
Introduce a discipline	7.6%	6.9%
Other*	14.7%	4.3%

Note. Percentages do not equal 100%. Respondents were asked to select three most important objectives.
*$p < .05$
**$p < .01$

Table 7.80
Most Important Course Objectives by Institutional Selectivity (N = 621)

	High (*n* = 56)	Other (*n* = 565)
Develop academic skills**	80.4%	61.8%
Orient to campus resources and services	26.8%	62.8%
Encourage self-exploration/personal development**	19.6%	41.8%
Develop support network/friendships*	21.4%	38.6%
Create common first-year experience	41.1%	35.6%
Increase student/faculty interaction**	60.7%	28.3%
Improve sophomore return rates**	3.6%	29.0%
Introduce a discipline*	16.1%	6.4%
Other**	26.8%	7.8%

Note. Percentages do not equal 100%. Respondents were asked to select three most important objectives.
*$p < .05$
**$p < .01$

Table 7.81

Most Important Course Objectives by Seminar Type (N = 621)

	EO	AUC	AVC	BSS	PRE	Other
	(*n* = 303)	(*n* = 120)	(*n* = 102)	(*n* = 34)	(*n* = 17)	(*n* = 17)
Develop academic skills**	55.8%	70.0%	76.5%	94.1%	35.3%	66.7%
Orient to campus resources & services**	80.2%	41.7%	21.6%	52.9%	52.9%	66.7%
Encourage self-exploration /personal development**	43.6%	47.5%	20.6%	52.9%	23.5%	37.0%
Develop support network/friendships**	45.5%	25.8%	26.5%	35.3%	17.7%	40.7%
Create common first-year experience**	30.4%	56.7%	41.2%	17.7%	29.4%	29.6%
Increase student/ faculty interaction**	22.8%	26.7%	57.8%	21.0%	41.2%	51.9%
Improve sophomore return rates	29.4%	19.2%	26.5%	41.2%	17.7%	25.9%
Introduce a discipline**	2.0%	7.5%	13.7%	2.9%	58.8%	0.0%
Other	4.3%	16.7%	17.7%	2.9%	17.7%	11.1%

Note. Percentages do not equal 100%. Respondents were asked to select three most important objectives.
**$p < .01$

Course Topics

The 2003 survey asked respondents to list the five most important topics in their first-year seminars. The five most frequently selected topics were study skills (62.8%), campus resources (61.5%), time management (59.7%), academic planning/advising (58.1%), and critical thinking (52.3%). Course topics varied greatly by seminar type. Critical thinking was selected most frequently by institutions offering primarily academic seminars—both those with uniform content (77.5%) and those with variable content (90.2%) across sections. Writing skills was also selected as an important topic by most institutions with primarily academic seminars with variable content (73.5%).

Study skills, campus resources, and time management were more often selected as important topics at public schools (71.9%, 69.3%, and 69.0%, respectively) than at private schools (53.8%, 53.8%, and 50.6%, respectively).

Highly selective schools were nearly twice as likely as other schools to select critical thinking as one of their five most important course topics (89.3% and 48.7%, respectively). College policies and procedures were considered one of the five most important seminar topics at less than 2% of the highly selective institutions, whereas 34.3% of other schools selected this topic (see Tables 7.82 - 7.85).

Table 7.82
Most Important Course Topics Across All Institutions (N = 621)

	Frequency	Percentage
Study skills	390	62.8
Campus resources	382	61.5
Time management	371	59.7
Academic planning/advising	361	58.1
Critical thinking	325	52.3
Career exploration/preparation	217	34.9
College policies & procedures	195	31.4
Writing skills	192	30.9
Diversity issues	186	30.0
Relationship issues	168	27.1
Specific disciplinary topic	125	20.1
Other	90	14.5

Note. Percentages do not equal 100%. Respondents were asked to select five items.

Table 7.83

Most Important Course Topics by Institutional Affiliation (N = 620)

	Private (n = 314)	Public (n = 306)
Study skills**	53.8%	71.9%
Campus resources**	53.8%	69.3%
Time management**	50.6%	69.0%
Academic planning/advising*	54.1%	62.4%
Critical thinking	55.1%	49.4%
Career exploration/preparation**	26.1%	44.1%
College policies & procedures	30.3%	32.7%
Writing skills**	37.3%	24.5%
Diversity issues	33.4%	26.1%
Relationship issues**	32.5%	21.6%
Specific disciplinary topic**	24.8%	15.4%
Other**	22.0%	6.9%

Note. Percentages do not equal 100%. Respondents were asked to select five items.
*p < .05
**p < .01

Table 7.84
Most Important Course Topics by Institutional Selectivity (N = 621)

	High (n = 56)	Other (n = 565)
Study skills**	28.6%	66.2%
Campus resources**	28.6%	64.8%
Time management**	14.3%	64.3%
Academic planning/advising**	41.1%	59.8%
Critical thinking**	89.3%	48.7%
Career exploration/preparation**	10.7%	37.4%
College policies & procedures**	1.8%	34.3%
Writing skills**	67.9%	27.3%
Diversity issues	41.1%	28.9%
Relationship issues**	7.1%	29.0%
Specific disciplinary topic**	55.4%	16.6%
Other**	33.9%	12.6%

Note. Percentages do not equal 100%. Respondents were asked to select five items.
**$p < .01$

Table 7.85
Most Important Course Topics by Seminar Type (N = 603)

	EO	AUC	AVC	BSS	PRE	Other
	(*n* = 303)	(*n* = 120)	(*n* = 102)	(*n* = 34)	(*n* = 17)	(*n* = 27)
Study skills**	75.2%	48.3%	40.2%	94.1%	35.3%	63.0%
Campus resources**	77.9%	41.7%	36.3%	50.0%	70.6%	59.3%
Time management**	78.2%	38.3%	21.6%	88.2%	58.8%	55.6%
Academic planning/ advising**	69.3%	44.2%	36.3%	58.8%	70.6%	55.6%
Critical thinking**	29.7%	77.5%	90.2%	61.8%	41.2%	59.3%
Career exploration/ preparation**	46.2%	26.7%	8.8%	29.4%	64.7%	29.6%
College policies & proceedures**	41.9%	22.5%	3.9%	38.2%	35.3%	37.0%
Writing skills**	12.9%	45.0%	73.5%	32.4%	17.6%	22.2%
Diversity issues**	25.1%	45.8%	33.3%	17.6%	29.4%	33.3%
Relationship issues**	33.3%	29.2%	11.8%	23.5%	5.9%	18.5%
Specific disciplinary topic**	2.3%	20.8%	71.6%	11.8%	47.1%	14.8%
Other**	9.6%	25.0%	20.6%	5.9%	5.9%	22.2%

Note. Percentages do not equal 100%. Respondents were asked to select five items.
**$p < .01$

Outcomes Attributed to Seminars

Our final survey question asked respondents to select from a list of potential results all the outcomes that could be attributed to student participation in their first-year seminars. Our statistics regarding seminar results must be tempered by the knowledge that only those institutions that had both assessed the particular outcome *and* found an improvement would have selected a specific response. Schools would be left out of this analysis if they had not done related assessment and/or if their assessment did not indicate improvement in a particular area.

Increased persistence to sophomore year and improved student connections with peers were reported by 58.7% and 58.4%, respectively, of institutions responding to this question. Student satisfaction with the institution and out-of-class student/faculty interaction were documented to have improved at over half of the responding institutions (51.2% and 50.6%, respectively). Differences in reported outcomes were apparent between public and private schools and between the different seminar types (see Tables 7.86 - 7.88). For additional information regarding assessment of first-year programs, see chapter 5.

Table 7.86
Results Attributed to First-Year Seminars Across All Institutions (N = 322)

	Frequency	Percentage
Improved or Increased:		
Persistence to sophomore year	189	58.7
Student connection with peers	188	58.4
Student use of campus services	165	51.2
Student satisfaction with the institution	163	50.6
Out-of-class student/faculty interaction	145	45.0
Level of student participation in campus activities	134	41.6
Academic abilities	116	36.0
Student satisfaction with faculty	100	31.1
Grade point average	86	26.7
Persistence to graduation	59	18.3

Note. Percentages do not equal 100%. Respondents could make more than one selection.

Table 7.87
Results Attributed to First-Year Seminars by Institutional Affiliation (N = 322)

	Private (*n* = 180)	Public (*n* = 142)
Improved or Increased:		
Persistence to sophomore year**	48.3%	71.8%
Student connection with peers	60.6%	55.6%
Student use of campus services	48.3%	54.9%
Student satisfaction with the institution	48.3%	53.5%
Out-of-class student/faculty interaction	47.8%	41.6%
Level of student participation in campus activities	42.8%	40.1%
Academic abilities*	31.1%	42.3%
Student satisfaction with faculty	30.6%	31.7%
Grade point average**	16.1%	40.1%
Persistence to graduation**	12.2%	26.1%
Other	11.7%	8.5%

Note. Percentages do not equal 100%. Respondents could make more than one selection.
*$p < .05$
**$p < .01$

Table 7.88
Results Attributed to First-Year Seminar by Seminar Type (N = 314)

	EO	AUC	AVC	BSS	PRE	Other
	(*n* = 159)	(*n* = 68)	(*n* = 49)	(*n* = 13)	(*n* = 10)	(*n* = 15)
Improved or Increased:						
Persistence to sophomore year	62.9%	51.5%	51.0%	84.6%	60.0%	53.3%
Student connection with peers	59.1%	52.9%	65.3%	46.2%	50.0%	66.7%
Student use of campus services**	65.4%	39.7%	26.5%	53.9%	30.0%	46.7%
Student satisfaction with the institution	51.6%	50.0%	44.9%	53.9%	60.0%	53.3%
Out-of-class student/ faculty interaction	40.9%	54.4%	49.0%	46.2%	20.0%	40.0%
Level of student participation in campus activities	45.3%	42.7%	34.7%	30.8%	0.0%	40.0%
Academic abilities**	27.7%	39.7%	55.1%	69.2%	40.0%	13.3%
Student satisfaction with faculty	25.2%	25.0%	51.0%	38.5%	40.0%	26.7%
Grade point average	33.3%	17.7%	16.3%	53.9%	10.0%	20.0%
Persistence to graduation	18.2%	17.6%	14.3%	38.5%	10.0%	20.0%
Other	7.6%	11.8%	14.3%	0.0%	30.0%	13.3%

Note. Percentages do not equal 100%. Respondents could make more than one selection.
**$p < .01$

Notes

[1]We compared highly selective institutions with all others. *Peterson's 2004 Four Year Colleges* defines "highly selective" as institutions that are the "most difficult or very difficult" to get in.

Summary of Selected Findings

8

The monograph, as a whole, is designed to draw a detailed portrait of the structure, administration, and instruction of first-year seminars on the campuses of participating institutions. Up to this point, the monograph has focused on specific aspects of first-year seminars from unique curricular interventions to a comparison between institutional types. It has provided a comprehensive collection of tables reflecting all significant survey results. To complete the portrait, this chapter provides an overview of survey findings, including a trends analysis of survey results from the first survey administration in 1988 to the present. Thus, the seminar portrait is complete.

Selected Key Findings

These findings come from the 2003 aggregated data of not-for-profit institutions offering first-year seminars. This is not an exhaustive list, but hopefully one that captures the current state of the seminar. The findings are described with reference to the course, the students, the instructors, and the course administration.

The Course

- The most common type of seminar at reporting institutions was the extended orientation seminar. More than 65% of all institutions reported offering this type of seminar.
- Seminar classes tended to be small. The section size for approximately 87% of the seminars across institution type was between 10 and 25 students.
- The most common course objectives across all institutions and seminar types were to develop academic skills (63.5%), provide orientation to campus resources and services (59.6%), and encourage self-exploration/personal development (39.8%).
- The most common course topics across all institutions and seminar types were study skills (62.8%), campus resources (61.5%), time management (59.7%), academic planning and advising (58.1%), and critical thinking (52.3%).
- More than three quarters of all institutions reported offering the seminar for a letter grade (78.8%).
- In almost 90% of the institutions, students could earn academic credit for the seminar. In almost half of the institutions, the course carried one credit (49.5%). In almost one third of the institutions, the course carried three credits (31.2%).
- Almost one quarter of participating institutions reported they have a service-learning component as a part of their seminar (23.7%).

- Almost one quarter of the reporting institutions offered the first-year seminar as part of a learning community (24.8%).

The Students

- The seminar was required for all students in almost 50% of the reporting institutions. Approximately 20% of the institutions did not require it of any of their first-year students.
- When the seminar was required, it was most frequently (20.7%) required for provisionally admitted students.
- Special sections of the seminar were offered at over 50% of all participating institutions. More than 20% of the institutions offered special sections for academically underprepared students, and almost 20% of the institutions reported offering special sections for their honors students.

The Instructors

- At approximately 90% of institutions, faculty taught the first-year seminar. For most of the faculty, teaching the seminar was part of their regular teaching load.
- At 76.2% of the institutions, student affairs professionals and other campus professionals taught the first-year seminar. For most administrators, teaching the seminar was an extra responsibility (58.9%).
- In most cases, when the seminar was an extra duty, instructors received a stipend (74.6%). The stipend amount ranged from $250-$5,400, with an average of approximately $1,250 per section, and a modal response of $500. Some institutions gave more money to experienced faculty, while others did not report the amount, saying it was tied to credit hours (i.e., the more credit attached to the seminar, the more the instructor was paid).
- Nearly 40% of reporting institutions offered at least one team-taught section. At approximately one quarter of these institutions (26.6%), all sections were team taught.
- Almost one third of the reporting institutions assigned students to sections taught by their academic advisors (30.4%). This occurred more frequently in highly selective institutions (i.e., those identified by *Peterson's 2004 Four-Year Colleges* as institutions that are the "most difficult" and "very difficult" to get in) (44.6% vs. 29% for all other institutions) and in private institutions (36.1% vs. 24.7% in public institutions).
- Most institutions participating in the survey offered instructor training (72.4%) and of those institutions, 68.8% required first-year seminar instructor training.
- Instructor training tended to last two days or less in 76.8% of those participating institutions offering training.

The Administration

- Academic affairs was the unit most frequently responsible for administering the seminar (46.2%).
- Most participating institutions had a director or coordinator for the seminar (77.3%), and this person was full-time at 34% of all those institutions.
- Only 8.7% of the institutions reported offering their course for two years or less; 50.2% have offered the course for 3 to 10 years; and 41.1% reported offering their course for more than 10 years.

Trends

Table 8.1 reflects the general response rate for the 2003 survey as it compares to previous administrations. It is important to remember that this survey is dramatically different from previous years[1] and that some variation exists in the list of participating institutions from year to year. Therefore, it is impossible to determine change over time or draw any direct comparisons. Rather, the survey iterations provide snapshots in time regarding the status of the first-year seminar as reflected by the responding institutions. Thus, it is still possible to see trends among participating institutions over the years. Table 8.2 reflects those trends.

Table 8.1

Comparison of Institutions Offering First-Year Seminar, 1988-2003

Institutions offering a first-year seminar	Survey year					
	1988 ($N = 1,699$)	1991 ($N = 1,064$)	1994 ($N = 1,003$)	1997 ($N = 1,336$)	2000 ($N = 1,013$)	2003 ($N = 771$)
Number	1,163	695	720	939	749	629
Percentage	68.5	65.4	71.8	70.3	73.9	81.6

Note. 2003 survey underwent significant revisions and was administered via the web.

Table 8.2
Comparison of Survey Results, 1988-2003

Percentage of institutions that	Survey Year					
	1998 (N = 1,163)	1991 (N = 695)	1994 (N = 720)	1997 (N = 939)	2000 (N = 748)	2003 (N = 629)
Classify seminar type as						
Extended orientation		71.0	72.2	68.7	62.1	65.2
Academic (uniform content)		12.1	11.3	10.5	16.7	27.4
Academic (variable content)		7.0	7.8	9.7	12.8	24.3
Basic study skills		6.0	5.0	5.7	3.6	20.0
Pre-professional*		1.4	1.3	2.7	2.7	14.2
Other		3.8	3.8	2.7	2.1	8.2
Limit seminar size to 25 students	45.9*	68.1	59.8	68.4	47.5	86.9
Grade seminar with letter grade	61.9	68.1	75.4	76.6	81.7	78.9
Offer academic credit for seminar	82.2	85.6	86.1	87.8	90.0	89.3
Require seminar for all first-year students	43.5	45.0	42.8	46.9	49.7	46.8
Apply seminar credits as						
Core Requirements		19.4	18.9	19.8	22.0	
General Education		28.7	26.4	27.1	34.7	57.3
Elective		45.4	49.8	45.6	42.8	42.0
Major Requirement		2.4	1.5	3.1	4.8	6.0
Other		4.1	3.4	4.4	6.0	8.0
Provide seminar instruction using						
Faculty		84.5	85.0	87.0	88.9	89.9
Student affairs professionals		50.8	54.2	60.4	53.9	45.3
Other campus administrators		34.1	36.9	41.0	37.2	
Undergraduate students		8.1	8.6	9.0	10.0	6.3
Graduate students		4.2	5.8	6.0	4.9	4.4
Other		10.2	9.2	5.0	3.3	30.9

Table 8.2 (cont.)

Percentage of institutions that	Survey Year					
	1998 (N = 1,163)	1991 (N = 695)	1994 (N = 720)	1997 (N = 939)	2000 (N = 748)	2003 (N = 629)
Use seminar instructors to advise their seminar students					20.1	30.4
Assign teaching of seminar as						
Regular load for faculty		51.9	53.2	55.4	57.8	68.8**
Overload for faculty		36.5	38.2	42.8	40.1	39.6**
Regular load for administrators		25.2	28.2	25.7	24.8	41.7**
Extra responsibility for administrators		31.7	29.4	36.2	34.8	58.9**
Offer training for instructors		71.4	70.8	75.9	77.2	72.4
Require training for instructors		46.7	48.2	49.6	49.4	68.8**
Linkage to learning community			17.2	14.1	25.1	24.8
Report program longevity as						
2 years or less	30.1	23.8	22.4	16.7	11.7	8.7
10 years or less		81.4	80.9	72.3	79.1	58.9
Over 10 years						41.1

Note. Blank fields reflect questions not on survey or posed in different manner.
* Seminar limited to fewer than 20 students.
** The total population (*N*) reflects the number of institutions with seminars responding to the survey. The 2003 survey provided follow-up questions for sub-populations, (e.g., overload and regular load questions were not posed to general population, only to those institutions that use faculty as instructors). Therefore, the number reported reflects the percentage of that sub-group that responded; it does not reflect the percentage of the general population.

Many features of first-year seminars have remained relatively stable over each of the six survey administrations. These features include:

- *Seminar type.* More than two thirds of participating institutions offered extended orientation seminars (range 62.1% to 72.2%).
- *Instruction.* A majority of institutions used faculty as seminar instructors and about half of the institutions used student affairs professionals as instructors (range of 84.5% to 89.9%).
- *Credit.* Among our survey participants, the seminar almost always carried academic credit (range of 82.2% to 90%).

- *Required status.* Through the years, almost half of all participating institutions required all first-year students to take the seminar (range of 42.8% to 49.7%).
- *Links to other courses.* Almost a quarter of our participating institutions in 2000 and 2003 reported that the first-year seminar was part of a learning community (25.1% and 24.8% respectively). This is up from previous survey administrations.

Thus, even though many elements of the seminar seem to be undergoing changes, several elements remain consistent over the years among respondents.

Conclusion

Our primary goal with this monograph was to give information that can be used to help establish or refine first-year seminars. Though course elements may change over time, the ultimate objective that drives all our efforts is to help first-year students succeed. We hope that this monograph has provided readers with valuable insights into the first-year seminar as it exists on participants' campuses today and that this information helps readers in their efforts to support first-year students.

Notes

[1]Several categories are not reported in the table, because the wording of the question is different or the question no longer exists in the latest version of the survey. This is the case for course objectives/goals, course topics, and institutional support. However, we did include the most recent data in previous chapters or the summary in this chapter.

References

Peterson's Four-Year Colleges 2004. (34th ed.). (2003). Lawrenceville, NJ: Thomson-Peterson's.

Appendix

Survey Instrument

The following survey does not reflect the layout of the web-based survey but accurately captures the content of those questions. In the web administration, follow-up questions were prompted by specific answers, but here all questions, including the follow-ups, are listed.

2003/04 National Survey on First-Year Seminars
National Resource Center for The First-Year Experience & Students in Transition
University of South Carolina

This survey is dedicated to gathering information regarding first-year seminars. First-year seminars are courses designed to enhance the academic skills and/or social development of first-year college students.

The survey should take approximately 15 minutes to complete and, once started, cannot be saved for completion at a later time. Your responses are important to us. Therefore, please allot 15-20 minutes to respond by November 21, 2003. Thank you.

Does your institution (including any department or division) offer one or more first-year seminar type courses?   Yes _____   No _____

Background Information

Name of institution _____

Your name _____   Title _____

Department address _____

City _____   State _____   Zip code _____

Telephone _____   E-mail _____

Mark appropriate categories regarding your institution:

Two-year institution_____   Four-year institution_____

Public_____   Private_____   Proprietary_____

Quarter system _____   Semester system_____

1. What is the approximate undergraduate enrollment (head count) at your institution? _____

2. What is the approximate number of entering first-year students at your institution? _____

3. Does your institution (including any department or division) offer one or more first-year seminar-type courses?   Yes_____   No_____

Types of Seminars Offered

4. Approximately how many years has a first-year seminar been offered on your campus?   _____ years

5. What is the approximate percentage of first-year students who participate in a first-year seminar course? _____

6. Select each *discrete* type of first-year seminar that best describes the seminars that exist on your campus.

　　a._____ Extended orientation seminar. Sometimes called freshman orientation, college survival, college transition, or student success course. Content likely will include introduction to campus resources, time management, academic and career planning, learning strategies, and an introduction to student development issues.

　　b._____ Academic seminar with generally uniform academic content across sections. May be an interdisciplinary or theme-oriented course, sometimes part of a general education requirement. Primary focus is on academic theme/discipline, but will often include academic skills components such as critical thinking and expository writing.

　　c._____ Academic seminars on various topics. Similar to previously mentioned academic seminar except that specific topics vary from section to section.

　　d._____ Pre-professional or discipline-linked seminar. Designed to prepare students for the demands of the major/discipline and the profession. Generally taught within professional schools or specific disciplines such as engineering, health sciences, business, or education.

　　e._____ Basic study skills seminar. Offered for academically underprepared students. The focus is on basic academic skills such as grammar, note-taking, and reading texts, etc.

　　f. _____ Other
Describe: _____

_____

Specific Seminar Information

7. If you offer more than one first-year seminar type, select the **seminar type with the highest total student enrollment** to answer the remaining questions. That seminar type is:

_____Extended orientation seminar
_____Academic seminar with generally uniform content
_____Academic seminar on various topics
_____Pre-professional or discipline-linked seminar
_____Basic study skills seminar
_____Other

8. Please indicate the approximate number of sections of this seminar type offered in the 2003/2004 academic year: _____

Please answer the remaining questions for the seminar type with the highest student enrollment.

The Students

9. What is the approximate class size for each first-year seminar section?

_____ Under 10 students
_____ 10 - 15
_____ 16 - 20
_____ 21 - 25
_____ Other   Specify: _____

10. What is the approximate percentage of first-year students *required* to take the first-year seminar?

_____ 100%	_____ 79 - 70%	_____ less than 50%
_____ 99 - 90%	_____ 69 - 60%	_____ 0%
_____ 89 - 80%	_____ 59 - 50%	

11. If less that 100%, which students (by category) are *required* to take the first-year seminar? (Select all that apply.)

_____ None are required to take it
_____ Honors students
_____ Learning community participants
_____ Provisionally admitted students
_____ Student athletes
_____ Students in specific majors (List the majors_____)
_____ Undeclared students
_____ Other Describe: _____

12. Are special sections of the first-year seminar offered for any of the following unique sub-populations of students? (Select all that apply.)

       ____ No special sections are offered
       ____ Academically underprepared students
       ____ Honors students
       ____ International students
       ____ Learning community participants
       ____ Pre-professional students (i.e., pre-law, pre-med)
       ____ Students residing within a particular residence hall
       ____ Students within a specific major (Please list the majors_____)
       ____ Transfer students
       ____ Undeclared students
       ____ Other

The Instructors

13. Who teaches the first-year seminar? (Select all that apply.)

       _____ Faculty
       _____ Graduate students
       _____ Undergraduate students
       _____ Student affairs professionals
       _____ Other campus professionals Describe: _____

14. How are undergraduate students used in the first-year seminar? (Select all that apply.)

       _____They teach independently.
       _____They teach as part of a team.
       _____They assist the instructor.

15. Are any first-year students intentionally placed in first-year seminar sections taught by their academic advisors?   Yes_____ No_____
If yes, give the approximate percentage of students placed in sections with their academic advisors _____

16. Are any sections of the course team taught?   Yes_____ No _____

17. Indicate the approximate percentage of sections that are team taught.

       _____100%
       _____99 - 75%
       _____74 - 50%
       _____49 - 25%
       _____Less than 25%

18. Please identify team configurations used in your first-year seminar courses. _____

19. For faculty, how is teaching the first-year seminar configured for workload? (Select all that apply.)
   _____ As part of regular teaching load
   _____ As an overload course
   _____ Other Describe:_____

20. For administrative staff, how is teaching the first-year seminar configured for workload? (Select all that apply.)
   _____ As one of the assigned responsibilities
   _____ As an extra responsibility
   _____ Other Describe:_____

21. If taught as an overload or extra responsibility, what type of compensation is offered for teaching a first-year seminar? Please mark all that apply and provide a description of each compensation in the accompanying text box.
   _____ Stipend   Specify:_____
   _____ Release time Specify:_____
   _____ Graduate student support Specify: _____
   _____ Other   Specify:_____

22. Is instructor training *offered* for first-year seminar instructors?
   Yes_____   No _____

23. If yes, how long is instructor training?
   ____ Half a day or less   _____ 3 days   _____Other
   ____ 1 day   _____ 4 days   Describe: _____
   ____ 2 days   _____ 1 week

24. Is instructor training *required* for first-year seminar instructors?
   Yes _____   No _____

The Course

25. Is this first-year seminar offered for:
   _____ One semester
   _____ One quarter
   _____ Other Describe: _____

26. How is the first-year seminar graded?
   ____ Pass/fail
   ____ Letter grade
   ____ No grade

27. How many total classroom contact hours are there per week in the first-year seminar?
   _____ One   _____ Three   _____ Five
   _____ Two   _____ Four   _____ More than five

28. Does the first-year seminar carry academic credit?
   Yes _____   No _____

29. How many credits does the first-year seminar carry? (Select all that apply.)

_____ One   _____ Three   _____ Five

_____ Two   _____ Four   _____ More than five

30. How does such credit apply? (Select all that apply.)

____ As an elective

____ Toward general education requirements

____ Toward major requirements

____ Other Describe: _____

31. Does the first-year seminar include a service-learning component (non-remunerative service as part of a course)? Yes_____   No _____

If yes, describe: _____

32. Is the first-year seminar linked to one or more other courses (i.e., "learning community" – enrolling a cohort of students into two or more courses)?

Yes_____   No_____

If yes, describe: _____

33. Select **THREE** of the most important course objectives for this first-year seminar.

____Create common first-year experience

____Develop academic skills

____Develop support network/friendships

____Improve sophomore return rates

____Increase student/faculty interaction

____Introduce a discipline

____Provide orientation to campus resources and services

____Self-exploration/personal development

____Other Describe: _____

34. Select **FIVE** of the most important topics that comprise the content of this first-year seminar.

____Academic planning/advising

____Career exploration/preparation

____Campus resources

____College policies and procedures

____Critical thinking

____Diversity issues

____Relationship issues (e.g., interpersonal skills, conflict resolution)

____Specific disciplinary topic

____Study skills

____Time management

____Writing skills

____Other Describe: _____

35. Please list up to three elements or aspects of your first-year seminar that you consider **innovative or especially successful.**

_____

_____

_____

36. Is part or all of this first-year seminar taught online?
Yes _____   No _____
If yes, describe those elements: _____

The Administration

37. What campus unit directly administers the first-year seminar?
____Academic affairs
____Academic department   Specify: _____
____First-year program office
____Student affairs
____Other   Describe: _____

38. Is there a director/coordinator of the first-year seminar?
        Yes_____   No _____

39. If yes, is this position
        _____ Full time (approximately 40 hours per week)
        _____ Less than full-time

40. If less than 40 hours, how many hours per week? _____

41. If less than 40 hours, does the director/coordinator have another position on campus? Yes _____   No _____

42. The director/coordinator's other campus role is as a/an:
        _____ Academic affairs administrator
        _____ Faculty member
        _____ Student affairs administrator
        _____ Other Describe:_____

Evaluation Results

43. Has a formal program evaluation been conducted on your first-year seminar since fall 2000?   Yes _____   No _____

44. If yes, what type of evaluation was conducted? (Select all that apply.)

_____Focus groups with instructors
_____Focus groups with students
_____Individual interviews with instructors
_____Individual interviews with students
_____Student course evaluation
_____Survey instrument
_____Use of collected institutional data
_____Other   Describe:._____

45. Did your institution create the survey instrument?

Yes_____   No_____

46. Did your institution use an established instrument?

Yes_____   No_____

47. List instruments used:

_____ First-Year Initiative (FYI)
_____ Your First College Year (YFCY)
_____ Other   Specify:_____

48. Through your formal evaluation efforts, which of the following results can be attributed to participation in your first-year seminar? (Select all that apply.)

_____Improved connections with peers
_____Improved grade point average
_____Increased academic abilities
_____Increased level of student participation in campus activities
_____Increased out-of-class interaction with faculty
_____Increased persistence to sophomore year
_____Increased persistence to graduation
_____Increased student satisfaction with faculty
_____Increased student satisfaction with the institution
_____Increased use of campus services
_____Other   Describe: _____

Survey Responses

It is our practice to make available to all requesting institutions specific and general information gathered from this survey. Please let us know if we can share your specific survey information with others by selecting the appropriate response below:

_____You may share my survey responses.
_____Please do not share my survey responses.

Appendix

Respondents to the 2003 National Survey on First-Year Seminars

Non-Proprietary Institutions[1]

Abilene Christian University	Abilene	TX
Adams State College	Alamosa	CO
Alabama A&M University	Normal	AL
Alderson-Broaddus College	Philippi	WV
Alexandria Technical College	Alexandria	MN
Alice Lloyd College	Pippa Passes	KY
Alliant International University	San Diego	CA
Angelina College	Lufkin	TX
Anne Arundel Community College	Arnold	MD
Antioch College	Yellow Springs	OH
Arizona State University West	Phoenix	AZ
Arkansas Baptist College	Little Rock	AR
Arkansas State University	State University	AR
Armstrong Atlantic State University	Savannah	GA
Asbury College	Wilmore	KY
Asheville-Buncombe Technical Community College	Asheville	NC
Ashland Community and Technical College	Ashland	KY
Assumption College for Sisters	Mendham	NJ
Atlantic Union College	South Lancaster	MA
Aurora University	Aurora	IL
Avila University	Kansas City	MO
Baker College of Muskegon	Muskegon	MI
Baker University	Baldwin City	KS
Barat College of Depaul University	Lake Forest	IL
Bard College	Annandale	NY
Barnard College	New York	NY
Barton College	Wilson	NC
Barton County Community College	Great Bend	KS
Baruch College	New York	NY
Bates College	Lewiston	ME
Bellevue Community College	Bellevue	WA
Belmont University	Nashville	TN
Beloit College	Beloit	WI
Bentley College	Waltham	MA

Bergen Community College	Paramus	NJ
Berry College	Mount Berry	GA
Bethany Lutheran Collegwe	Mankato	MN
Bethel College	North Newton	KS
Bethel College	McKenzie	TN
Biola University	La Mirada	CA
Bloomfield College	Bloomfield	NJ
Boise State University	Boise	ID
Boston College	Chestnut Hill	MA
Bowling Green State University	Bowling Green	OH
Bowling Green State University Firelands College	Huron	OH
Bradley University	Peoria	IL
Brazosport College	Lake Jackson	TX
Brewton-Parker College	Mt. Vernon	GA
Briar Cliff University	Sioux City	IA
Briarwood College	Southington	CT
Brigham Young University-Hawaii	Laie	HI
Bristol Community College	Fall River	MA
Bronx Community College	Bronx	NY
Brooklyn College	Brooklyn	NY
Brown University	Providence	RI
Bryant College	Smithfield	RI
Buena Vista University	Storm Lake	IA
Burlington College	Burlington	VT
Caldwell College	Caldwell	NJ
California State University, Bakersfield	Bakersfield	CA
California State University, Chico	Chico	CA
California State University, Fullerton	Fullerton	CA
California State University, Long Beach	Long Beach	CA
California State University, Los Angeles	Los Angeles	CA
California State University, Monterey Bay	Seaside	CA
California State University, Northridge	Northridge	CA
California State University, Sacramento	Sacramento	CA
California State University, San Bernardino	San Bernardino	CA
Calvary Bible College	Kansas City	MO
Calvin College	Grand Rapids	MI
Campbell University	Buies Creek	NC
Canisius College	Buffalo	NY
Cankdeska Cikana Community College	Fort Totten	ND
Cape Cod Community College	W. Barnstable	MA
Capitol College	Laurel	MD
Carroll College	Helena	MT
Carroll Community College	Westminster	MD

Carteret Community College	Morehead City	NC
Castleton State College	Castleton	VT
Catawba Valley Community College	Hickory	NC
Cayuga Community College	Auburn	NY
Cazenovia College	Cazenovia	NY
Cedarville University	Cedarville	OH
Central Baptist College	Damascus	AR
Central Florida Community College	Ocala	Fl
Central Lakes College	Brainerd	MN
Central Missouri State University	Warrensburg	MO
Central Piedmont Community College	Charlotte	NC
Central State University	Wilberforce	OH
Chaminade University of Honolulu	Honolulu	HI
Chattahoochee Valley Community College	Phenix City	AL
Chestnut Hill College	Philadelphia	PA
Claremont McKenna College	Claremont	CA
Clarion University of Pennsylvania	Clarion	PA
Clarkson College	Omaha	NE
Clemson University	Clemson	SC
Cleveland Community College	Shelby	NC
Cleveland State University	Cleveland	OH
Cloud County Community College	Concordia	KS
Cochise College	Douglas	AZ
Coconino Community College	Flagstaff	AZ
Colby Community College	Colby	KS
College for Creative Studies	Detroit	MI
College of Biblical Studies-Houston	Houston	TX
College of Mount St. Joseph	Cincinnati	OH
College of Notre Dame of Maryland	Baltimore	MD
College of Saint Mary	Omaha	NE
College of Santa Fe	Santa Fe	NM
College of Southern Idaho	Twin Falls	ID
College of Staten Island	Staten Island	NY
College of the Mainland	Texas City	TX
College of William and Mary	Williamsburg	VA
Colorado College	Colorado Springs	CO
Colorado State University-Pueblo	Pueblo	CO
Columbia College	Columbia	SC
Columbus College of Art and Design	Columbus	OH
Community College of Denver	Denver	CO
Community College of Southern Nevada	Las Vegas	NV
Conception Seminary College	Conception	MO

Concordia College	Bronxville	NY
Concordia University	River Forest	IL
Concordia University Wisconsin	Mequon	WI
Concordia University, St. Paul	St. Paul	MN
Converse College	Spartanburg	SC
Cornell College	Mount Vernon	IA
Cornerstone University	Grand Rapids	MI
Corning Community College	Corning	NY
Cossatot Community College of the University of Arkansas	De Queen	AR
Crafton Hills College	Yucaipa	CA
Craven Community College	New Bern	NC
Crossroads College	Rochester	MN
Cuesta College	San Luis Obispo	CA
Cumberland College	Williamsburg	KY
Cumberland County College	Vineland	NJ
Cumberland Universtiy	Lebanon	TN
Curry College	Milton	MA
Cuyahoga Community College	Cleveland	OH
Dallas Christian College	Dallas	TX
Daniel Webster College	Nashua	NH
Dartmouth College	Hanover	NH
Darton College	Albany	GA
Davenport University	Dearborn	MI
Dean College	Franklin	MA
Delaware State University	Dover	DE
Delgado Community College	New Orleans	LA
Delta State University	Cleveland	MS
Denison University	Granville	OH
DePaul University	Chicago	IL
Dickinson College	Carlisle	PA
D-Q University	Davis	CA
Drake University	Des Moines	IA
Drew University	Madison	NJ
Drury University	Springfield	MO
Duke University	Durham	NC
Duquesne University	Pittsburgh	PA
Dutchess Community College	Poughkeepsie	NY
East Tennessee State University	Johnson City	TN
East Texas Baptist University	Marshall	TX
Eastern Illinois University	Charleston	IL
Eastern Kentucky University	Richmond	KY
Eastern New Mexico University, Roswell	Roswell	NM
Eastern Wyoming College	Torrington	WY

Edgecombe Community College	Tarboro	NC
Elizabeth City State University	Elizabeth City	NC
Elms College	Chicopee	MA
Elon University	Elon	NC
Embry-Riddle Aeronautical University	Prescott	AZ
Endicott College	Beverly	MA
Erskine College	Due West	SC
Essex County College	Newark	NJ
Eugenio Marìa de Hostos Community College of City University of New York	Bronx	NY
Evangel University	Springfield	MO
Finlandia University	Hancock	MI
Fitchburg State College	Fitchburg	MA
Florida College	Temple Terrace	FL
Florida Gulf Coast University	Ft. Myers	FL
Florida Institute of Technology	Melbourne	FL
Florida Memorial College	Miami	FL
Fond du Lac Tribal and Community College	Cloquet	MN
Fort Lewis College	Durango	CO
Fox Valley Technical College	Appleton	WI
Franciscan University of Steubenville	Steubenville	OH
Franklin College	Franklin	IN
Fresno Pacific University	Fresno	CA
Fullerton College	Fullerton	CA
Genesee Community College	Batavia	NY
Georgetown College	Georgetown	KY
Georgia Military College	Milledgeville	GA
Georgia State University	Atlanta	GA
Germanna Community College	Locust Grove	VA
Goucher College	Baltimore	MD
Grand Valley State University	Allendale	MI
Grand View College	Des Moines	IA
Grinnell College	Grinnell	IA
Gustavus Adolphus College	St. Peter	MN
Hampshire College	Amherst	MA
Harrisburg Area Community College	Harrisburg	PA
Haskell Indian Nations University	Lawrence	KS
Heartland Community College	Normal	IL
Hebrew College	Newton	MA
Helene Fuld College of Nursing	New York	NY
Henderson Community College	Henderson	KY
Henderson State University	Arkadelphia	AR
Herkimer County Community College	Herkimer	NY

Hiwassee College	Madisonville	TN
Hobart and William Smith Colleges	Geneva	NY
Hocking College	Nelsonville	OH
Holy Cross College	Notre Dame	IN
Holyoke Community College	Holyoke	MA
Hood College	Frederick	MD
Hope International University	Fullerton	CA
Hudson Valley Community College	Troy	NY
Hunter College	New York	NY
Huntingdon College	Montgomery	AL
Huntington College	Huntington	IN
Idaho State University	Pocatello	ID
Illinois College	Jacksonville	IL
Illinois State University	Normal	IL
Indian Hills Community College	Ottumwa	IA
Indiana Institute of Technology	Fort Wayne	IN
Indiana University Kokomo	Kokomo	IN
Indiana University Southeast	New Albany	IN
Indiana University-Purdue University Indianapolis	Indianapolis	IN
Inter-American University of Puerto Rico Aguadilla Campus	Aguadilla	PR
International College	Naples	FL
Inver Hills Community College	Inver Grove Heights	MN
Isothermal Community College	Spindale	NC
Ithaca College	Ithaca	NY
Jackson State Community College	Jackson	TN
James Madison University	Harrisonburg	VA
Jewish Hospital College	St. Louis	MO
John A. Logan College	Carterville	IL
John Carroll University	University Heights	OH
John Jay College of Criminal Justice, CUNY	New York	NY
Johnson County Community College	Overland Park	KS
Joliet Junior College	Joliet	IL
Juniata College	Huntingdon	PA
Kalamazoo College	Kalamazoo	MI
Kapi'olani Community College	Honolulu	HI
Kennesaw State University	Kennesaw	GA
Kentucky State University	Frankfort	KY
Keuka College	Keuka Park	NY
Keystone College	La Plume	PA
Kilgore College	Kilgore	TX
King College	Bristol	TN

King's College	Wilkes-Barre	PA
Kingsborough Community College	Brooklyn	NY
Knox College	Galesburg	IL
Labette Community College	Parsons	KS
LaGuardia Community College	Long Island City	NY
Lamar University	Beaumont	TX
Lander University	Greenwood	SC
Las Positas College	Livermore	CA
Lasell College	Newton	MA
Lee University	Cleveland	TN
Lees-McRae College	Banner Elk	NC
Lehman College	Bronx	NY
Lexington Community College	Lexington	KY
Lincoln Memorial University	Harrogate	TN
Lindenwood University	St. Charles	MO
Lindsey Wilson Colelge	Columbia	KY
Little Big Horn College	Crow Agency	MT
Little Priest Tribal College	Winnebago	NE
Lon Morris College	Jacksonville	TX
Longwood University	Farmville	VA
Lord Fairfax Community College	Middletown	VA
Louisburg College	Louisburg	NC
Louisiana State University at Eunice	Eunice	LA
Louisiana State University at Shreveport	Shreveport	LA
Lower Columbia College	Longview	WA
Loyola College in Maryland	Baltimore	MD
Loyola University Chicago	Chicago	IL
Lycoming College	Williamsport	PA
Lynn University	Boca Raton	FL
Macalester College	St. Paul	MN
Madison Area Technical College	Madison	WI
Madonna University	Livonia	MI
Maine College of Art	Portland	ME
Manatee Community College	Bradenton	FL
Manchester Community College	Manchester	CT
Marist College	Poughkeepsie	NY
Martin Luther College	New Ulm	MN
Martin Methodist College	Pulaski	TN
Mary Washington College	Fredericksburg	VA
Maryland College of Art and Design	Silver Spring	MD
Marymount University	Arlington	VA
Maryville College	Maryville	TN
Massachusetts College of Art	Boston	MA

Massachusetts College of Pharmacy and Health Sciences	Boston	MA
Mayville State University	Mayville	ND
McDaniel College	Westminster	MD
McKendree College	Lebanon	IL
Meridian Community College	Meridian	MS
Mesa State College	Grand Junction	CO
Metropolitan State College of Denver	Denver	CO
Metropolitan University, Ana G. Mendez University System	San Juan	PR
MidAmerica Nazarene University	Olathe	KS
Middlesex Community College	Middletown	CT
Millersville University	Millersville	PA
Millsaps College	Jackson	MS
Milwaukee Institute of Art & Design	Milwaukee	WI
Minneapolis Community and Technical College	Minneapolis	MN
Minnesota School of Business	Richfield	MN
Minot State University-Bottineau	Bottineau	ND
Missouri Western State College	St. Joseph	MO
Mohave Community College	Kingman	AZ
Montreat College	Montreat	NC
Moore College of Art & Design	Philadelphia	PA
Moraine Valley Community College	Palos Hills	IL
Moravian College	Bethlehem	PA
Morehead State University	Morehead	KY
Morningside College	Sioux City	IA
Morris College	Sumter	SC
Mount Marty College	Yankton	SD
Mount St. Mary's College	Emmitsburg	MD
Mountain State University	Beckley	WV
Mt. San Jacinto College	San Jacinto	CA
Muskegon Community College	Muskegon	MI
Muskingum Area Technical College	Zanesville	OH
Nassau Community College	Garden City	NY
Nazareth College of Rochester	Rochester	NY
Neumann College	Aston	PA
New England School of Communications	Bangor	ME
New Mexico Highlands University	Las Vegas	NM
New Mexico Junior College	Hobbs	NM
New Orleans Baptist Theological Seminary	New Orleans	LA
New York City College of Technology	Brooklyn	NY
New York Institute of Technology	Old Westbury	NY
Niagara University	Niagara University	NY

Nichols College	Dudley	MA
Norfolk State University	Norfolk	VA
Normandale Community College	Bloomington	MN
North Central Missouri College	Trenton	MO
North Central State College	Mansfield	OH
North Central Texas College	Gainesville	TX
North Dakota State College of Science	Wahpeton	ND
North Florida Community College	Madison	FL
North Idaho College	Coeur d'Alene	ID
Northeastern Oklahoma A&M College	Miami	OK
Northeastern University	Boston	MA
Northern State University	Aberdeen	SD
Northland College	Ashland	WI
Northwest Arkansas Community College	Bentonville	AR
Northwest College	Powell	WY
Northwestern Oklahoma State University	Alva	OK
Northwood University	Midland	MI
Notre Dame College	South Euclid	OH
Nunez Community College	Chalmette	LA
Occidental College	Los Angeles	CA
Ohio Dominican University	Columbus	OH
Ohio University Chillicothe	Chillicothe	OH
Ohio University Southern	Ironton	OH
Ohio Valley College	Vienna	WV
Oklahoma Wesleyan University	Bartlesville	OK
Olivet Nazarene University	Bourbonnais	IL
Oregon State University	Corvallis	OR
Ouachita Technical College	Malvern	AR
Our Lady of Holy Cross College	New Orleans	LA
Pacific Lutheran University	Tacoma	WA
Pacific States University	Los Angeles	CA
Pacific University	Forest Grove	OR
Palo Alto College	San Antonio	TX
Panola College	Carthage	TX
Parker College of Chiropractic	Dallas	TX
Paul Quinn College	Dallas	TX
Paul Smith's College	Paul Smiths	NY
Penn State Abington	Abington	PA
Penn State Berks, Lehigh Valley College	Reading	PA
Penn State, Capital College	Middletown	PA
Penn State Delco	Media	PA
Penn State Erie, The Behrend College	Erie	PA
Penn State University	University Park	PA

Penn State, York	York	PA
Pennsylvania College of Art & Design	Lancaster	PA
Pennsylvania College of Technology	Williamsport	PA
Peru State College	Peru	NE
Pfeiffer University	Misenheimer	NC
Philander Smith College	Little Rock	AR
Phoenix College	Phoenix	AZ
Pillsbury Baptist Bible College	Owatonna	MN
Pine Manor College	Chestnut Hill	MA
Plattsburgh State University of New York	Plattsburgh	NY
Plymouth State University	Plymouth	NH
Point Loma Nazarene University	San Diego	CA
Pontifical Catholic University of Puerto Rico	Mayaguez	PR
Pontifical Catholic University of Puerto Rico, Ponce Campus	Ponce	PR
Porterville College	Porterville	CA
Portland State University	Portland	OR
Presbyterian College	Clinton	SC
Pulaski Technical College	North Little Rock	AR
Purdue University North Central	Westville	IN
Queens College, City University of New York	Flushing	NY
Queensborough Community College	Bayside	NY
Quincy College	Quincy	MA
Quinebaug Valley Community College	Danielson	CT
Radford University	Radford	VA
Randolph Community College	Asheboro	NC
Raritan Valley Community College	Somerville	NJ
Reed College	Portland	OR
Reformed Bible College	Grand Rapids	MI
Rend Lake College	Ina	IL
Rhodes State College	Lima	OH
Richard Bland College of The College of William and Mary	Petersburg	VA
Richland Community College	Decatur	IL
Rider University	Lawrenceville	NJ
Ripon College	Ripon	WI
Riverland Community College	Austin	MN
Roanoke Bible College	Elizabeth City	NC
Robert Morris University	Moon Township	PA
Rochester Institute of Technology	Rochester	NY
Rockford College	Rockford	IL
Rocky Mountain College	Billings	MT
Rogers State University	Claremore	OK

Rollins College	Winter Park	FL
Russell Sage College	Troy	NY
Sacred Heart University	Fairfield	CT
St. Ambrose University	Davenport	IA
St. Gregory's University	Shawnee	OK
Saint Joseph College	West Hartford	CT
Saint Joseph's College	Rensselaer	IN
St. Lawrence University	Canton	NY
Saint Leo University	Saint Leo	FL
St. Louis College of Pharmacy	St. Louis	MO
St. Mary's University	San Antonio	TX
Saint Paul's College	Lawrenceville	VA
Saint Xavier University	Chicago	IL
Salisbury University	Salisbury	MD
Salve Regina University	Newport	RI
Samford University	Birmingham	AL
San Diego State University	San Diego	CA
San Francisco Art Institute	San Francisco	CA
San Jacinto College North	Houston	TX
San Juan College	Farmington	NM
Santa Ana College	Santa Ana	CA
Santa Rosa Junior College	Santa Rosa	CA
Santiago Canyon College	Orange	CA
Savannah State University	Savannah	GA
School of the Museum of Fine Arts, Boston	Boston	MA
Schreiner University	Kerrville	TX
Seton Hall University	South Orange	NJ
Seward County Community College	Liberal	KS
Shelton State Community College	Tuscaloosa	AL
Shepherd College	Shepherdstown	WV
Simpson College	Indianola	IA
Smith College	Northampton	MA
South Central Technical College	North Mankato	MN
South Dakota School of Mines and Technology	Rapid City	SD
Southeast Missouri State University	Cape Girardeau	MO
Southeastern Bible College	Birmingham	AL
Southeastern Louisiana University	Hammond	LA
Southern Arkansas University	Magnolia	AR
Southern Virginia University	Buena Vista	VA
Southwest Missouri State University	Springfield	MO
Southwest Mississippi Community College	Summit	MS
Southwest Tennessee Community College	Memphis	TN
Southwestern Illinois College	Belleville	IL

Southwestern University	Georgetown	TX
Spartanburg Technical College	Spartanburg	SC
Spencerian College	Lexington	KY
Spring Hill College	Mobile	AL
Stanford University	Stanford	CA
Stark State College of Technology	Canton	OH
State University of New York at Cortland	Cortland	NY
State University of New York at Maritime	Bronx	NY
Stephens College	Columbia	MO
Stony Brook University	Stony Brook	NY
Suffolk County Community College	Selden	NY
Sussex County Community College	Newton	NJ
Sweet Briar College	Sweet Briar	VA
Syracuse University	Syracuse	NY
Tabor College	Hillsboro	KS
Tarleton State University	Stephenville	TX
Teikyo Post University	Waterbury	CT
Texas A&M University-Kingsville	Kingsville	TX
Texas Lutheran University	Seguin	TX
Texas State Technical College – Harlingen	Harlingen	TX
The City College of New York	New York	NY
The College of St. Benedict & St. John's University	St. Joseph & Collegeville	MN
The College of Wooster	Wooster	OH
The Cooper Union for the Advancement of Science and Art	New York	NY
The Ohio State University	Columbus	OH
The Richard Stockton College of New Jersey	Pomona	NJ
The University of South Dakota	Vermillion	SD
The University of Tennessee	Knoxville	TN
The University of Texas at Austin	Austin	TX
The University of West Alabama	Livingston	AL
Thomas More College	Crestview Hills	KY
Thomas University	Thomasville	GA
Towson University	Towson	MD
TransPacific Hawaii College	Honolulu	HI
Trinity Christian College	Palos Heights	IL
Trinity College	Hartford	CT
Tri-State University	Angola	IN
Truckee Meadows Community College	Reno	NV
Tulane University	New Orleans	LA
Turtle Mountain Community College	Belcourt	ND
Union College	Schenectady	NY

Union College	Barbourville	KY
Union University	Jackson	TN
Unity College	Unity	ME
Universidad del Sagrado Corazon	San Juan	PR
University of Arkansas - Fort Smith	Fort Smith	AR
University of California, Irvine	Irvine	CA
University of California, Riverside	Riverside	CA
University of California, Santa Barbara	Santa Barbara	CA
University of Central Arkansas	Conway	AR
University of Central Oklahoma	Edmond	OK
University of Cincinnati	Cincinnati	OH
University of Dubuque	Dubuque	IA
University of Guam	Mangilao	Guam
University of Hawaii at Hilo	Hilo	HI
University of Judaism	Los Angeles	CA
University of Kentucky	Lexington	KY
University of La Verne	La Verne	CA
University of Maine at Augusta	Augusta	ME
University of Maine at Presque Isle	Presque Isle	ME
University of Mary Hardin-Baylor	Belton	TX
University of Massachusetts Amherst	Amherst	MA
University of Memphis	Memphis	TN
University of Michigan-Dearborn: College of Arts, Sciences, and Letters	Dearborn	MI
University of Minnesota, Morris	Morris	MN
University of Mobile	Mobile	AL
University of Montana - Helena College of Technology	Helena	MT
University of New Haven	West Haven	CT
University of New Mexico-Gallup	Gallup	NM
University of North Carolina at Chapel Hill	Chapel Hill	NC
University of North Carolina at Charlotte	Charlotte	NC
University of North Carolina at Greensboro	Greensboro	NC
University of Notre Dame	Notre Dame	IN
University of Oklahoma	Norman	OK
University of Oregon	Eugene	OR
University of Pittsburgh at Titusville	Titusville	PA
University of Portland	Portland	OR
University of Puerto Rico in Ponce	Ponce	PR
University of Richmond	Richmond	VA
University of San Diego	San Diego	CA
University of San Francisco	San Francisco	CA
University of Southern Maine	Portland	ME

University of St. Thomas	Saint Paul	MN
University of Tampa	Tampa	FL
University of Tennessee at Chattanooga	Chattanooga	TN
University of Texas at Tyler	Tyler	TX
University of Texas-Pan American	Edinburg	TX
University of the District of Columbia	Washington	DC
University of the Ozarks	Clarksville	AR
University of the Pacific	Stockton	CA
University of the Sciences in Philadelphia	Philadelphia	PA
University of Washington	Seattle	WA
University of Wisconsin-Eau Claire	Eau Claire	WI
University of Wisconsin-Green Bay	Green Bay	WI
University of Wisconsin-Milwaukee	Milwaukee	WI
University of Wisconsin-Oshkosh	Oshkosh	WI
University of Wisconsin-Parkside	Kenosha	WI
University of Wisconsin-Platteville	Platteville	WI
University of Wisconsin-Stout	Menomonie	WI
Ursinus College	Collegeville	PA
Ursuline College	Pepper Pike	OH
Utah State University	Logan	UT
University of Wisconsin-Parkside	Kenosha	WI
Valencia Community College	Orlando	FL
Valley Forge Military College	Wayne	PA
Vanderbilt University	Nashville	TN
Victor Valley College	Victorville	CA
Virginia Commonwealth University	Richmond	VA
Viterbo University	La Crosse	WI
Wabash College	Crawfordsville	IN
Wake Technical Community College	Raleigh	NC
Walsh University	North Canton	OH
Warren County Community College	Washington	NJ
Washington & Jefferson College	Washington	PA
Washington Bible College	Lanham	MD
Washington State University	Pullman	WA
Waukesha County Technical College	Pewaukee	WI
Waycross College	Waycross	GA
Wayland Baptist University	Plainview	TX
Webb Institute	Glen Cove	NY
Wells College	Aurora	NY
Wesley College	Dover	DE
Wesley College	Florence	MS
West Kentucky Community and Technical College	Paducah	KY

West Plains Campus, Southwest Missouri State University	West Plains	MO
West Virginia University	Morgantown	WV
Westchester Community College	Valhalla	NY
Western Baptist College	Salem	OR
Western Governors University	Salt Lake City	UT
Western Illinois University	Macomb	IL
Western Iowa Tech Community College	Sioux City	IA
Western Michigan University	Kalamazoo	MI
Western Piedmont Community College	Morganton	NC
Western State College	Gunnison	CO
Westfield State College	Westfield	MA
Westminster College	Fulton	MO
Westmoreland County Community College	Youngwood	PA
Wheaton College	Norton	MA
Wheeling Jesuit University	Wheeling	WV
Wilbur Wright College	Chicago	IL
William Jewell College	Liberty	MO
William Rainey Harper College	Palatine	IL
Wilson College	Chambersburg	PA
Windward Community College	Kane'ohe	HI
Wingate University	Wingate	NC
Winona State University	Winona	MN
Winston-Salem State University	Winston-Salem	NC
Wofford College	Spartanburg	SC
Worcester State College	Worcester	MA
Xavier University of Louisiana	New Orleans	LA
York College of the City University of New York	Jamaica	NY
York Technical College	Rock Hill	SC

Proprietary Institutions[2]

Bryant & Stratton College	Cleveland	OH
Bryant & Stratton College	Albany	NY
Bryant & Stratton College	Liverpool	NY
Daymar College	Owensboro	KY
DeVry University	Addison	IL
DeVry University-Colorado	Westminster	CO
DeVry University, Fremont College	Fremont	CA
Hamilton College	Urbandale	IA
Harrington College of Design	Chicago	IL
Heald College Salinas Campus	Salinas	CA
NTI School of CAD Technology	Eden Prairie	MN
Pittsburg Technical Institute	Oakdale	PA

| The Art Institute of Houston | Houston | TX |
| Utah Career College | West Jordan | UT |

Notes

[1] This is a partial list of respondents, as 143 non-proprietary schools asked not to be identified.

[2] This is a partial list of respondents. Seven proprietary schools asked not to be identified.

Appendix

Proprietary Institutions

For-profit institutions or proprietary or "career schools" are one of the fastest growing segments in higher education. These institutions focus on job training and skills leading to job advancement. According to the *Chronicle of Higher Education Almanac* (2003), there are 808 proprietary institutions, and 490 of those are two-year schools. Because of the growing impact of these institutions on the higher education landscape, the National Resource Center wanted to investigate the existence of first-year seminars in this educational sector. This was the first year we invited these institutions to participate in the survey and only a small percentage responded (21 institutions, eight with seminars). Given the low response rate, we cannot draw conclusions from these findings; nevertheless, the responses from the participating for-profit schools provide a glimpse into the use of first-year seminars on these campuses. Thus, we wanted to share this anecdotal information in the monograph.

Six of the responding for-profit institutions are four-year schools, and five are on the quarter system. All of the institutions have 5,000 or fewer students. Three of them reported that they have had a first-year seminar for two years or less, and four of the schools have had their seminar for 3 to10 years. In six of these schools, 76% to 100% of their students participated in their seminar. In all cases, the seminars were required of more than 60% of their students. The most prevalent types of seminars on these campuses were the extended orientation and the academic seminar with uniform content.

Faculty and student affairs professionals taught the sections at seven out of eight institutions. At one institution, representatives from the academic and financial aid office as well as the institutional technology office taught the seminar. In seven of the institutions, the seminar was part of the full-time faculty member's teaching load.

Six of the eight seminars were housed in either academic affairs or an academic department. One institution stated that their seminars were housed in student affairs. The seminar did not have a service-learning component at these institutions, and only one of these schools connected the seminar to a learning community. At this school, students went through their courses as a cohort, and the seminar was a part of that blocked programming.

As at other institutions, proprietary institutions offered a range of objectives for these seminars. Developing academic skills and providing a common first-year experience were the most frequently mentioned objectives in these cases. The seminars at proprietary institutions also covered a range of topics. Critical thinking and time management were the most common topics at six of the eight institutions. Only three of the eight institutions listed career exploration and planning as an important topic. Because proprietary institutions are generally considered to be career focused, it is surprising that only a few of the schools listed this as an important course topic.

These institutions described a number of practices that they deemed innovative or especially successful. For example, one college discussed how its location in Chicago proved a boon to their interior design students.

Four of the institutions have done formal evaluations since 2000, which primarily consisted of course evaluations. One institution conducted instructor focus groups, and one used institutional data to assess their seminars. With limited evaluation efforts, the outcomes were also limited. However, the most commonly cited outcomes were increased academic ability (three institutions) and increased satisfaction with the institution (three institutions). The outcomes matched the goals of the course, because developing academic skills and orienting the students to campus were important goals.

These findings begin to provide a glimpse into how the first-year seminar is used in proprietary institutions. Clearly, the small sample size makes these results somewhat circumspect. Nevertheless, this survey offers a first glimpse into the use of first-year seminars in this quickly expanding segment of higher education.

Reference

Almanac Issue 2003-2004. (2003, August 29). *The Chronicle of Higher Education*, p. 2.

About the Contributors

Barbara F. Tobolowsky is associate director of the National Resource Center for The First-Year Experience and Students in Transition. In this position, she has overall responsibility for the Center's research and publication efforts. Tobolowsky also teaches University 101 and graduate seminars in the Higher Education and Student Affairs program (HESA) at the University of South Carolina. She earned her doctorate from the University of California, Los Angeles, in higher education and organizational change.

Marla Mamrick is a research analyst for Student Affairs and Institutional Planning and Assessment at the University of South Carolina. She earned her master's of higher education and student affairs from the University of South Carolina where she received the Paul P. Fidler Award for research. Her current interests are enrollment management and higher education assessment.

Bradley E. Cox is the coordinator of research and public information at the National Resource Center for The First-Year Experience and Students in Transition. He earned his bachelor's degree from the University of North Carolina – Chapel Hill and completed his master's in higher education administration and student affairs at the University of South Carolina – Columbia. In his role at the Center, Cox is the editor of the First-Year Assessment (FYA) Listserv, an electronic magazine/listserv dedicated to assessment of the first college year. His personal research interests include residential colleges and faculty-student interaction outside of the classroom.

Other Titles on the First-Year Seminar and the First College Year

Monograph 42. *Exploring the Evidence, Volume III: Reporting Outcomes of First-Year Seminars.* Barbara F. Tobolowsky, Bradley E. Cox, and Mary T. Wagner, Editors. The third in a series of volumes reporting on the outcomes related to first-year seminars. Research from more than 30 institutions is collected here. Each report includes descriptions of the institution and its students, the seminar course, research methods, and course outcomes. Reported course outcomes are related to retention, student learning and engagement, interaction with faculty, social integration, satisfaction with the institution, and GPA. Both quantitative and qualitative research reports are included. (2005). $35.00

Monograph 40. *The 2003 Your First-College Year (YFCY) Survey: Exploring the Academic and Personal Experiences of First-Year Students.* Jennifer R. Keup and Ellen Bara Stolzenberg. Keup and Stolzenberg report findings from a relatively new and unique instrument which paint a portrait of the cognitive and affective development of first-year students who entered college in fall 2002. The monograph includes a description of the first-year experience by key subgroups (commuter and residential populations are included) and provides an analysis of students' development over the course of the first year. Offers strategies for using these findings to provide intentional, effective initiatives on individual campuses. (2004). $35.00

Monograph 37. *Proving and Improving, Volume II: Tools and Techniques for Assessing the First College Year.* Randy L. Swing, Editor. Produced in association with the Policy Center on the First Year of College. This second volume of *Proving and Improving* collects essays from the First-Year Assessment Listserv, which is hosted by the Policy Center on the First Year of College and the National Resource Center. Like the first volume, this one brings together the nation's leading experts and practitioners of assessment in the first college year. They offer overviews of commercially available instruments and provide case studies of qualitative assessment strategies. Strategies for implementing an effective assessment effort and a typology of assessment instruments are also included. (2001). $35.00

Monograph 33. *Proving and Improving: Strategies for Assessing the First College Year.* Randy L. Swing, Editor. Drawn from the First-Year Assessment Listserv, which is hosted by the Policy Center on the First Year of College and the National Resource Center, this collection provides essays by the nation's best theorists and practitioners of first-year college assessment. Contributors outline the essentials of effective assessment efforts, provide a philosophical rationale for those essentials, describe methods and strategies for assessment, and provide examples designed for institutions and specific programs. (2001). $20.00

Monograph 25. *Exploring the Evidence, Volume II: Reporting Outcomes of First-Year Seminars.* Betsy O. Barefoot, Carrie Warnock, Michael Dickinson, Sharon Richardson, and Melissa Roberts, Editors. Produced with the financial support of the Houghton Mifflin Company. Reviews research outcomes of 50 first-year seminars, including improved retention and graduation rates, higher grade point averages, increased levels of student satisfaction, and improved teaching strategies. (1998). $30.00

Use this form to order additional copies of this monograph or to order other titles from the National Resource Center for The First-Year Experience & Students in Transition.

Prices advertised in this publication are subject to change.

Item	Quantity	Price	Total
Monograph 41. *The 2003 National Survey on First-Year Seminars*		$35.00	
Monograph 42. *Exploring the Evidence, Volume III*		$35.00	
Monograph 40. *The 2003 Your First College Year (YCFY) Survey*		$30.00	
Monograph 37. *Proving and Improving, Volume II*		$35.00	
Monograph 33. *Proving and Improving, Volume I*		$20.00	
Monograph 25. *Exploring the Evidence, Volume II*		$30.00	

Shipping Charges:

	Order Amount	Shipping Cost
U.S.	$1 - $50	$ 6.50 US
	$51 - $150	$10.00 US
	over $150	$15.00 US

Foreign — For orders shipped outside of the United States, customers will be billed exactshipping charges plus a $5.00 processing fee. Fax or e-mail us to obtain a shipping estimate. Be sure to include a list of items you plan to purchase and to specify your preference for Air Mail or UPS Delivery.

Shipping & Handling

Total

Name _____ Department _____

Institution _____ Telephone _____

Address _____

City _____ State/Province _____ Postal Code _____

E-mail Address _____

Select your option payable to the University of South Carolina:

❏ Check Enclosed   ❏ Institutional Purchase Order   Purchase Order No. _____

Credit Card: ❏ VISA   ❏ MasterCard   ❏ DISCOVER

Card No. _____ Expiration Date _____

Name of Cardholder _____

Billing Address _____

City _____ State/Province _____ Postal Code _____

Signature _____

Mail this form to: National Resource Center for The First-Year Experience & Students in Transition, University of South Carolina, 1728 College Street, Columbia, SC 29208. Phone (803) 777-6229. FAX (803) 777-4699.
E-mail burtonp@sc.edu Federal ID 57-6001153.